THE CHRISTMAS HANDBOOK

BY
MALC°LM BIRD & ALAN DART

M

MACMILLAN CHILDREN'S BOOKS

Copyright © Text & ideas Malcolm Bird and Alan Dart 1986
Copyright © Illustrations – Malcolm Bird 1986

All rights reserved.

First published in Great Britain 1986 by Pavilion Books Limited
Produced by David Booth (Publishing) Limited

Premier Picturemac edition published 1989 by
Macmillan Children's Books
A division of Macmillan Publishers Limited
London and Basingstoke
Associated companies throughout the world

ISBN 0-333-516257

A CIP catalogue record for this book is available from the British Library

Printed in Italy

FOR MY DEAR PARENTS, PHYL AND JOHN DART, WITH VERY BEST LOVE AND THANKS FOR MAKING EVERY CHRISTMAS SPECIAL. A.D.

FOR MY PARENTS – EDNA AND GEOFF BIRD, WHO FIRST INTRODUCED ME TO CHRISTMAS. MUCH LOVE AND THANKS FOR ALWAYS ENCOURAGING ME TO DRAW. M.B.

CONTENTS

Chapter 1	What Is Christmas?	7
Chapter 2	Countdown To Christmas	11
Chapter 3	Outside In The Snow	23
Chapter 4	Yuletide Fashion	27
Chapter 5	Decorations And Wrapping	35
Chapter 6	The Christmas Tree	43
Chapter 7	Father Christmas	51
Chapter 8	Festive Fare	59
Chapter 9	Christmas Fun And Games	67
Chapter 10	After Christmas	79
Chapter 11	Christmas Around The World	83
Chapter 12	Twelfth Night	91
Index		95

CHAPTER 1

What is Christmas?

What is Christmas?

DO YOU REMEMBER WHEN OUR MOTHERS TOOK US TO SEE FATHER CHRISTMAS AT THE STORE?

YES — I LOVED PICKING A PRESENT FROM THE LUCKY DIP BARREL — YOU NEVER KNEW WHAT YOU'D GET

YOU AND NOEL WERE THE BEST OF FRIENDS EVEN THEN

...AND THEN THERE WAS THAT SPECIAL CHRISTMAS WHEN WE GOT MARRIED

WE EVEN GAVE YOU BOTH CHRISTMASSY NAMES BECAUSE IT'S OUR FAVOURITE TIME OF YEAR

YOU DON'T KNOW WHAT CHRISTMAS IS ALL ABOUT YET, DO YOU?

NOW THAT'S THE REAL MEANING OF CHRISTMAS!

CHAPTER 2

Countdown to Christmas

Advent Crowns

The four weeks leading up to Christmas are called Advent, and start on the Sunday nearest to 30th November. They symbolise the coming of Christ, the fourth week never being completed to signify that His coming will never cease. Advent used to be a period of fasting, but is now more popularly regarded as the countdown to Christmas, when preparations are made for the holidays. A traditional way to celebrate the four Sundays of Advent is to make an Advent crown, a wreath of greenery bearing four candles. On the first Sunday in Advent the first candle on the crown is lit, to be joined by the second candle on the next Sunday, until all four candles are lit on the last Sunday before Christmas. Here we have three variations on the same theme – Candle Wreath is the old-fashioned Advent crown; Glitter Stars is re-usable and represents the Star of Bethlehem, with four smaller stars to add each Sunday; Tinsel Dome bears card candles, making it a safe version of the traditional crown.

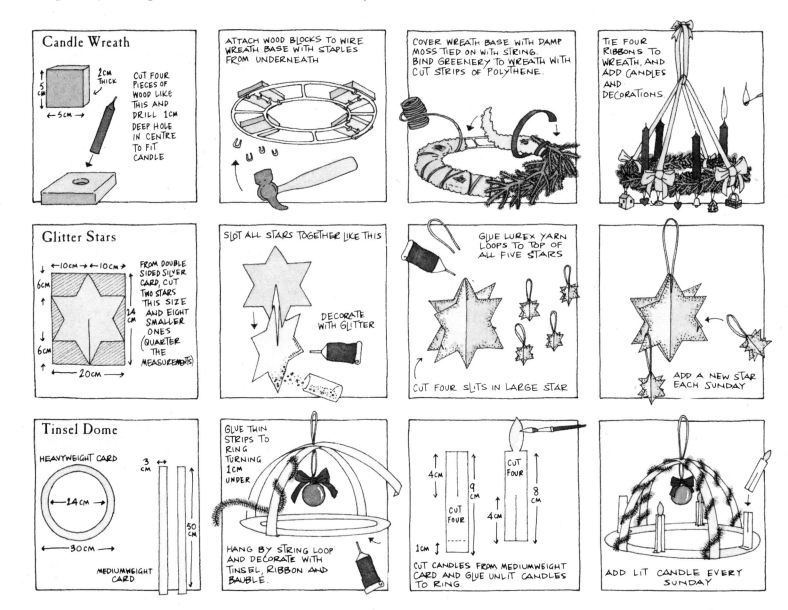

Candle Wreath

2CM THICK · 5 CM · 5CM
CUT FOUR PIECES OF WOOD LIKE THIS AND DRILL 1CM DEEP HOLE IN CENTRE TO FIT CANDLE

ATTACH WOOD BLOCKS TO WIRE WREATH BASE WITH STAPLES FROM UNDERNEATH

COVER WREATH BASE WITH DAMP MOSS TIED ON WITH STRING. BIND GREENERY TO WREATH WITH CUT STRIPS OF POLYTHENE.

TIE FOUR RIBBONS TO WREATH, AND ADD CANDLES AND DECORATIONS.

Glitter Stars

10CM · 10CM · 6CM · 24CM · 6CM · 20CM
FROM DOUBLE SIDED SILVER CARD, CUT TWO STARS THIS SIZE AND EIGHT SMALLER ONES (QUARTER THE MEASUREMENTS)

SLOT ALL STARS TOGETHER LIKE THIS
DECORATE WITH GLITTER

GLUE LUREX YARN LOOPS TO TOP OF ALL FIVE STARS
CUT FOUR SLITS IN LARGE STAR

ADD A NEW STAR EACH SUNDAY

Tinsel Dome

HEAVYWEIGHT CARD
14 CM · 30 CM
3 CM
50 CM
MEDIUMWEIGHT CARD

GLUE THIN STRIPS TO RING TURNING 1CM UNDER
HANG BY STRING LOOP AND DECORATE WITH TINSEL, RIBBON AND BAUBLE.

4CM · 9 CM · CUT FOUR · 1CM · CUT FOUR · 4CM · 8 CM
CUT CANDLES FROM MEDIUMWEIGHT CARD AND GLUE UNLIT CANDLES TO RING.

ADD LIT CANDLE EVERY SUNDAY

Advent Calendars

Another way to count the days leading up to Christmas is by using an Advent calendar. The type most commonly known is that of a scene, printed on card, with twenty-four small numbered windows which are opened each day to reveal a picture. Another version is an Advent candle, which is marked in twenty-four sections and lit every day, burning that day's portion. You can easily make your own Advent candle by marking and numbering a thick candle with enamel paint and a fine paintbrush, adding painted stars or holly leaves to

decorate. The three calendars shown here can be kept and used each year, with fresh cookies and treats added. Cookie Tree holds twenty-four cookies which have been numbered with icing, and hung by yarn threaded through a hole made in each cookie before baking; Puzzle Blocks is in the form of a jigsaw, and can be made in any size from Christmas card to wall poster; Treat Tree could hold small bath oil pearls, or miniature toys, instead of sweets . . . or a mixture of all three.

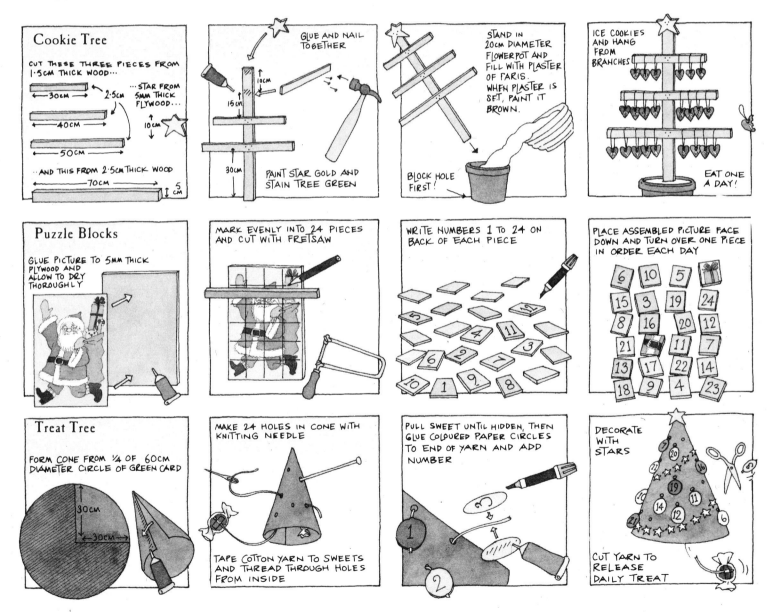

Christmas Cards
Origami Father Christmas

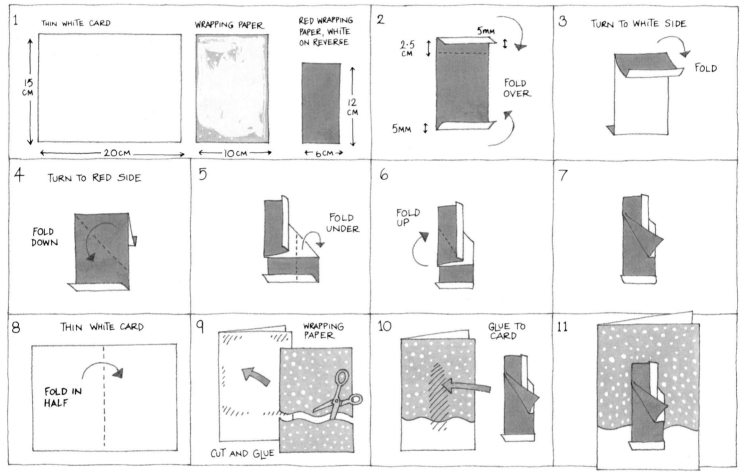

Stained Glass Window

Tissue Paper Christmas Tree

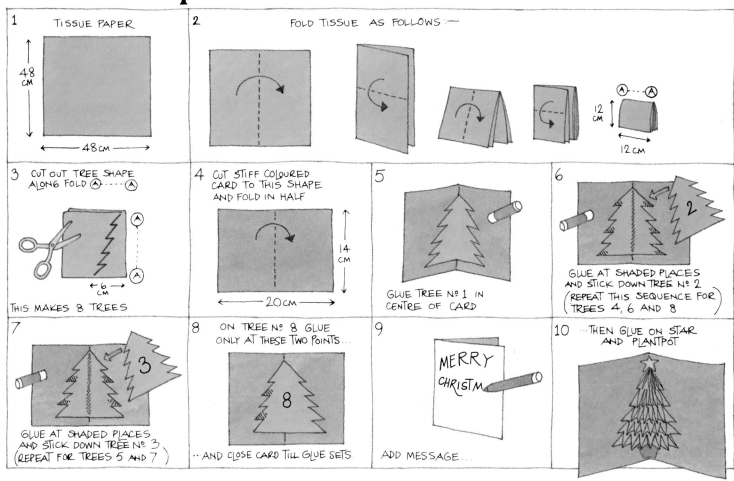

1 TISSUE PAPER
48 CM
48 CM

2 FOLD TISSUE AS FOLLOWS:—
12 CM
12 CM
A····A

3 CUT OUT TREE SHAPE ALONG FOLD Ⓐ····Ⓐ
6 CM
THIS MAKES 8 TREES

4 CUT STIFF COLOURED CARD TO THIS SHAPE AND FOLD IN HALF
14 CM
20 CM

5 GLUE TREE Nº 1 IN CENTRE OF CARD

6 2 GLUE AT SHADED PLACES AND STICK DOWN TREE Nº 2 (REPEAT THIS SEQUENCE FOR TREES 4, 6 AND 8)

7 3 GLUE AT SHADED PLACES AND STICK DOWN TREE Nº 3 (REPEAT FOR TREES 5 AND 7)

8 ON TREE Nº 8 GLUE ONLY AT THESE TWO POINTS...
8
...AND CLOSE CARD TILL GLUE SETS.

9 MERRY CHRISTM
ADD MESSAGE...

10 ...THEN GLUE ON STAR AND PLANTPOT

Christmas Cracker

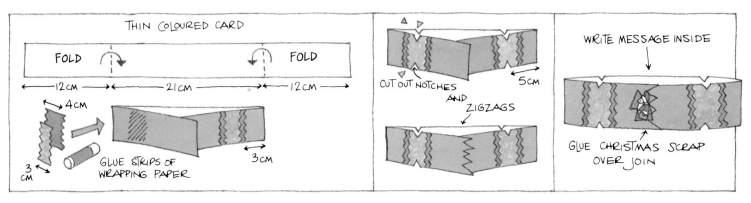

THIN COLOURED CARD
FOLD   FOLD
12 CM   21 CM   12 CM

4 CM
3 CM
GLUE STRIPS OF WRAPPING PAPER
3 CM

CUT OUT NOTCHES AND ZIGZAGS
5 CM

WRITE MESSAGE INSIDE
GLUE CHRISTMAS SCRAP OVER JOIN

Handmade Gifts
Grandma Ivy Makes Glove Puppets

HOLLY AND ROBIN HAVE GONE OUT FOR A WALK - SO I'M MAKING THESE FOR THEIR CHRISTMAS PRESENTS

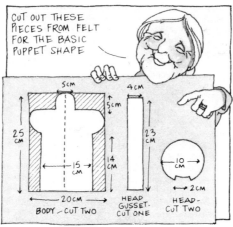

CUT OUT THESE PIECES FROM FELT FOR THE BASIC PUPPET SHAPE

5cm
5cm
4cm
25 CM
23 CM
14 CM
15 CM
20CM
10
2cm
BODY - CUT TWO
HEAD GUSSET - CUT ONE
HEAD - CUT TWO

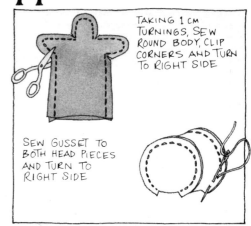

TAKING 1CM TURNINGS, SEW ROUND BODY, CLIP CORNERS AND TURN TO RIGHT SIDE

SEW GUSSET TO BOTH HEAD PIECES AND TURN TO RIGHT SIDE

PAD HEAD WITH STUFFING. PUSH NECK INTO HEAD, AND SEW ROUND BASE OF HEAD TO BODY.
NOW COMES THE FUN PART - MAKING DIFFERENT CHARACTERS!

25 cm
10CM
BEAD EYES

4
NOSE - GATHER FELT CIRCLE AND STUFF. SEW TO FACE

BEARD AND EYEBROWS FROM WADDING - GLUE TO FACE

EMBROIDER MOUTH

GLUE RIBBON BELT AND BUCKLE TO WAIST

CUT HOOD FROM FELT FOLD IN HALF AND SEW BACK SEAM TURN TO RIGHT SIDE. SEW ON BOBBLE AND GLUE ON STRIP OF FUR FABRIC. SEW HOOD TO HEAD

← GLUE ON FUR FABRIC STRIPS

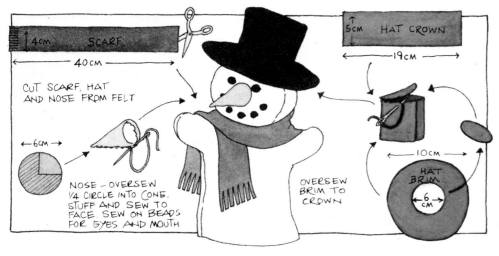

4cm
SCARF
40cm
6cm

5CM
HAT CROWN
19CM

CUT SCARF, HAT AND NOSE FROM FELT

NOSE - OVERSEW ¼ CIRCLE INTO CONE, STUFF AND SEW TO FACE. SEW ON BEADS FOR EYES AND MOUTH

OVERSEW BRIM TO CROWN

10CM
HAT BRIM
6 CM

ADD RIBBON AND BELL AT NECK

GLUE ON FELT EARS

SEW PIPECLEANER ANTLERS TO HEAD

SEW HEAD TO BODY WITH GUSSET AT FRONT

BEAD EYES

FELT NOSE

5CM

Grandpa Nicholas Makes a Book Stand

CAROL ALWAYS HAS TROUBLE PROPPING UP HER RECIPE BOOKS WHEN SHE'S COOKING — SO HERE'S A PRESENT TO SOLVE THAT!

25CM

2.5CM

B

A

30CM

DRAW PIECES Ⓐ AND Ⓑ ON 5MM THICK PLYWOOD AND CUT OUT — I'D USE A FRETSAW FOR PIECE Ⓐ

YOU'LL ALSO NEED PIECES Ⓒ AND Ⓓ

5 CM

1.5CM

C

25 CM

1CM DIAMETER DOWEL

15 CM

D

GLUE PIECE Ⓒ TO BASE OF BRANCHES ON PIECE Ⓐ

A

C

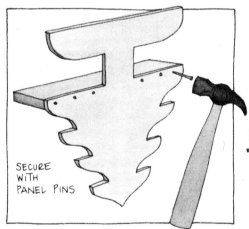

SECURE WITH PANEL PINS

GLUE AND PIN PLYWOOD PIECE Ⓑ TO FRONT OF BOOKREST

B

WITH 1CM DIAMETER DRILL, MAKE HOLE 1.5CM DEEP THROUGH BACK INTO BOOKREST. PUSH DOWEL INTO HOLE.

SMOOTH ROUGH EDGES WITH SANDPAPER

DECORATE WITH PAINTED HEARTS AND STARS

PAINT WITH GREEN WOOD STAIN

FINISH WITH COAT OF CLEAR VARNISH

Carol Makes Bow Ties

NOEL DOESN'T OFTEN DRESS UP, BUT WHEN HE DOES HE LIKES TO WEAR A BOW TIE — HERE ARE THREE FOR HIM FOR CHRISTMAS

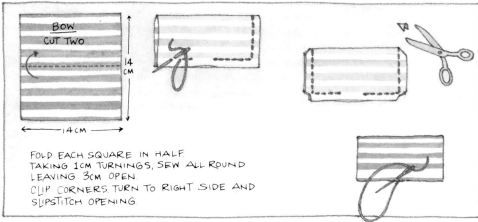

BOW
CUT TWO

14 CM

14CM

FOLD EACH SQUARE IN HALF
TAKING 1CM TURNINGS, SEW ALL ROUND
LEAVING 3CM OPEN.
CLIP CORNERS. TURN TO RIGHT SIDE AND
SLIPSTITCH OPENING.

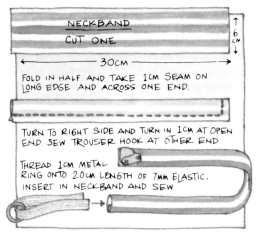

NECKBAND
CUT ONE

30CM

6 CM

FOLD IN HALF AND TAKE 1CM SEAM ON
LONG EDGE AND ACROSS ONE END.

TURN TO RIGHT SIDE AND TURN IN 1CM AT OPEN
END. SEW TROUSER HOOK AT OTHER END

THREAD 1CM METAL
RING ONTO 20CM LENGTH OF 7MM ELASTIC.
INSERT IN NECKBAND AND SEW

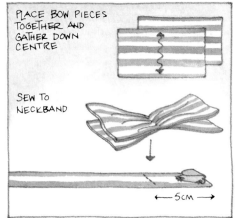

PLACE BOW PIECES
TOGETHER AND
GATHER DOWN
CENTRE

SEW TO
NECKBAND

5CM

4 CM

KNOT
CUT
ONE

6CM

FOLD UNDER 1CM
ON THREE SIDES.
WRAP ROUND BOW
AND STITCH TOGETHER
AT BACK.

HERE ARE TWO VARIATIONS TO MAKE!

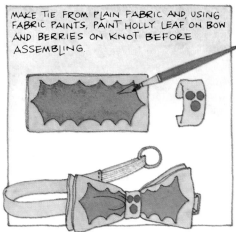

MAKE TIE FROM PLAIN FABRIC AND, USING
FABRIC PAINTS, PAINT HOLLY LEAF ON BOW
AND BERRIES ON KNOT BEFORE
ASSEMBLING.

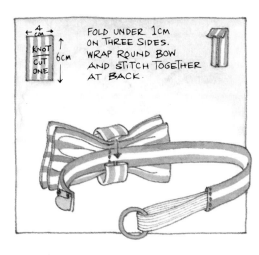

MAKE TIE FROM RED VELVET. DECORATE
WITH STRIPS OF FUR FABRIC MAKE KNOT
FROM BLACK SATIN AND ADD BUCKLE.

Noel Makes a Cheese Dish

GRANDPA NICHOLAS LOVES FOOD, SO I'M MAKING THIS CHEESE SAFE FOR HIM. IT'S BIG ENOUGH TO HOLD ALL HIS FAVOURITE CHEESES!

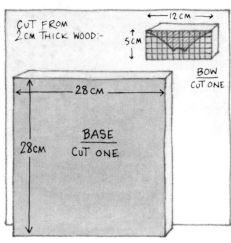
CUT FROM 2CM THICK WOOD:-

← 12CM →
5CM
BOW CUT ONE

28 CM
28CM
BASE CUT ONE

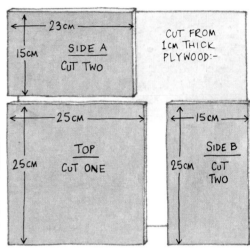
23CM
15CM
SIDE A CUT TWO

CUT FROM 1CM THICK PLYWOOD:-

25CM
25CM
TOP CUT ONE

15CM
25CM
SIDE B CUT TWO

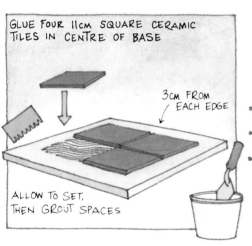
GLUE FOUR 11CM SQUARE CERAMIC TILES IN CENTRE OF BASE

3CM FROM EACH EDGE

ALLOW TO SET, THEN GROUT SPACES

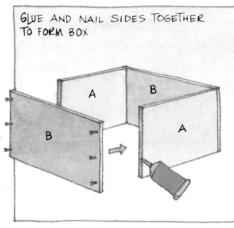
GLUE AND NAIL SIDES TOGETHER TO FORM BOX

A B
B A

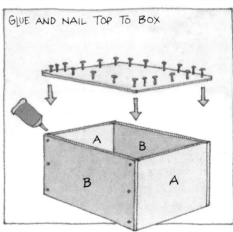
GLUE AND NAIL TOP TO BOX

A B
B A

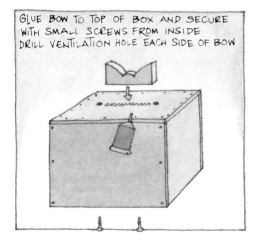
GLUE BOW TO TOP OF BOX AND SECURE WITH SMALL SCREWS FROM INSIDE DRILL VENTILATION HOLE EACH SIDE OF BOW

SAND EDGES AND PAINT WITH WOOD PRIMER

PAINT WITH ENAMEL PAINT AND DECORATE WITH PAINTED RIBBONS AND MOTIFS

Holly Makes a Bobble Robin

BABY LIKES PLAYING WITH WOOL BOBBLES, SO I'M MAKING A ROBIN BOBBLE FOR CHRISTMAS! FIRST I'LL SHOW YOU HOW TO MAKE A PLAIN ONE.

YOU'LL NEED TWO RINGS OF CARD AND SOME YARN.

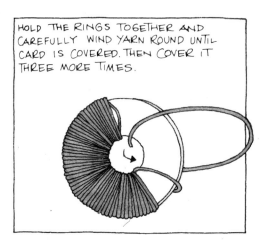

HOLD THE RINGS TOGETHER AND CAREFULLY WIND YARN ROUND UNTIL CARD IS COVERED. THEN COVER IT THREE MORE TIMES.

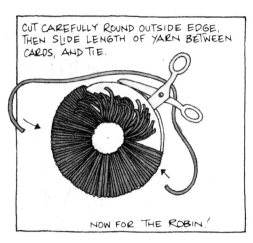

CUT CAREFULLY ROUND OUTSIDE EDGE, THEN SLIDE LENGTH OF YARN BETWEEN CARDS, AND TIE.

NOW FOR THE ROBIN!

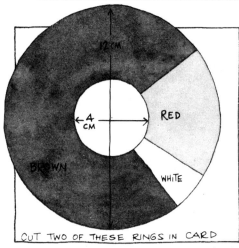

CUT TWO OF THESE RINGS IN CARD

WIND EACH SECTION SEPARATELY — I'VE DONE BROWN AND WHITE, SO FAR — RED'S NEXT!

REPEAT THREE MORE TIMES. CUT AND TIE AS I DEMONSTRATED EARLIER — I HOPE YOU WERE PAYING ATTENTION!

TRIM AWAY UNEVEN ENDS, THEN ADD BEAK, WINGS, TAIL AND EYES CUT FROM FELT (OR BEAD EYES IF FOR AN OLDER CHILD — ME, FOR INSTANCE!)

ON SECOND THOUGHT — PERHAPS BABY WOULD PREFER THE DEMONSTRATION MODEL!

Robin Makes Perfumed Treats

THESE ARE FOR GRANDMA IVY — FIRST TO MAKE IS A SIMMERING SPICE SACK — SHE CAN PUT ONE IN A PAN OF SIMMERING WATER TO SCENT THE WHOLE KITCHEN.

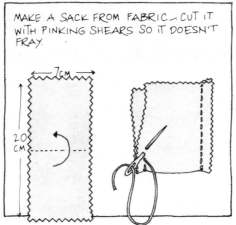

MAKE A SACK FROM FABRIC — CUT IT WITH PINKING SHEARS SO IT DOESN'T FRAY.

7 CM

20 CM

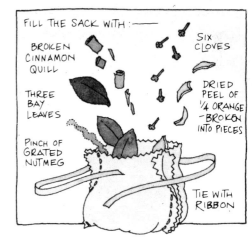

FILL THE SACK WITH : —

BROKEN CINNAMON QUILL

THREE BAY LEAVES

PINCH OF GRATED NUTMEG

SIX CLOVES

DRIED PEEL OF ¼ ORANGE — BROKEN INTO PIECES

TIE WITH RIBBON

TO MAKE A DRAWER SCENTER — CUT A RECTANGLE OF FABRIC

12 CM

20 CM

GLUE INTO TUBE WITH 1 CM OVERLAP

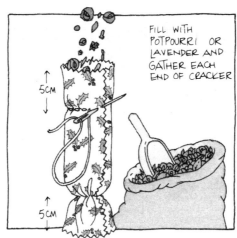

FILL WITH POTPOURRI OR LAVENDER AND GATHER EACH END OF CRACKER

5 CM

5 CM

GLUE ON RIBBON AND BOW — GRANDMA CAN PUT THIS BETWEEN THE CLOTHES IN HER DRAWER

NOW FOR A POMANDER — PIN TAPE ROUND ORANGE OR LEMON AND STUD WITH 30 G. OF CLOVES — MAKE HOLES WITH A KNITTING NEEDLE FIRST.

REMOVE TAPE. ROLL POMANDER IN 4 TABLESPOONS OF ORRIS ROOT POWDER — THIS FIXES THE SCENT. WRAP IN TISSUE AND KEEP IN WARM PLACE FOR THREE WEEKS.

TIE WITH RIBBON AND PLACE WITH THE OTHER TREATS — THEY'LL LOOK NICE IN THIS BASKET I'VE FOUND.

Choosing Presents

Each year we try to find new and exciting Christmas presents for our friends and relatives. A good starting point is to make a list of each person's interests and hobbies, and write down gift ideas that relate to them. Make sure that you buy clothes from a store that will exchange goods if they are the wrong size, or unsuitable. Some items, no matter how useful, can be too personal or boring to rate as presents . . . who wants a corset or a washing-up outfit for Christmas? A better idea is to give some little luxury – a special food or perfume – for a treat. It is not always necessary to spend a lot of money on gifts – often a child's drawing, or something handmade, can mean more than a shop-bought present. Don't forget that book, garden and gift vouchers can be the perfect answer for someone difficult. Below the Tinsel family show their reaction, good and bad, to their gifts.

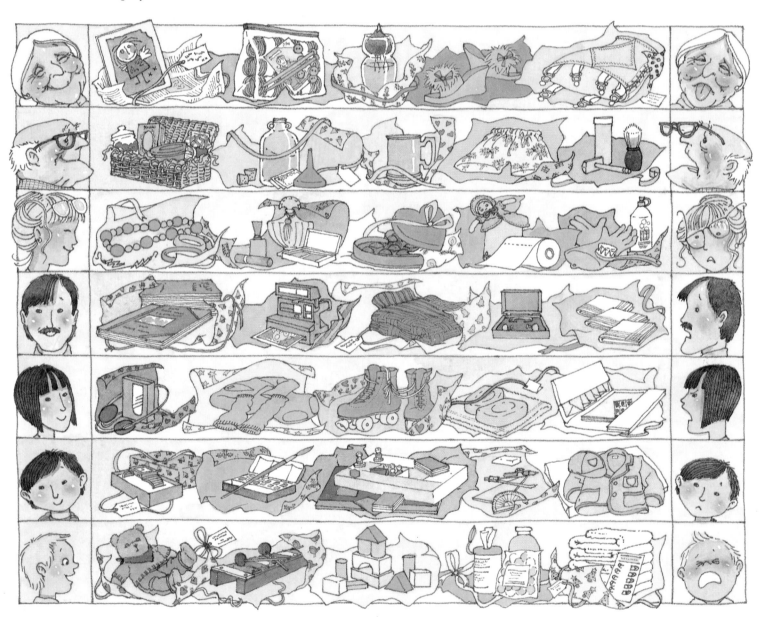

CHAPTER 3

Outside in the Snow

Snowfolk

Snowcastles

Angels in the Snow

Carol Singing

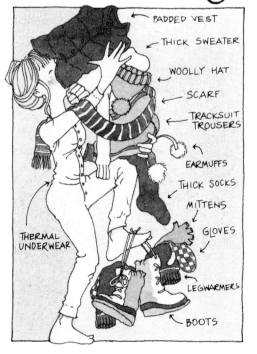

PADDED VEST

THICK SWEATER

WOOLLY HAT

SCARF

TRACKSUIT TROUSERS

EARMUFFS

THICK SOCKS

MITTENS

GLOVES

THERMAL UNDERWEAR

LEGWARMERS

BOOTS

HOTWATER BOTTLE

CANDLE IN JAMJAR

CAROLS

COLLECTING TIN

TORCH

HOT COCOA

MINCE PIES

PURSE

Evergreens

Rosemary is a symbol of friendship and remembrance. Said to have become scented when Christ's swaddling cloths were hung over it.

Holly leaves represent Christ's crown of thorns, and the berries the drops of blood. Guards against the evil eye.

Ivy is said to protect against the effects of drunkenness, and is a symbol of fertility as it refuses to die in winter.

Mistletoe stands for peace, protection and love. An old custom is to kiss under a sprig, picking a berry each time until all are gone.

CHAPTER 4

Yuletide Fashion

Father Christmas Outfit

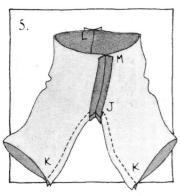

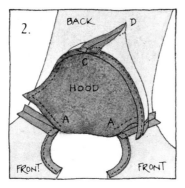

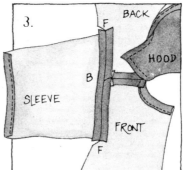

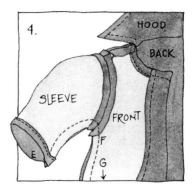

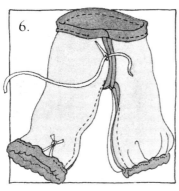

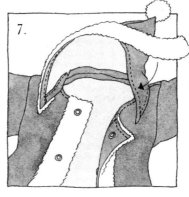

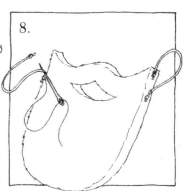

Christmas is Santa's busiest time of the year and he often needs help to hand out all the gifts that he has to deliver. His helpers are allowed to wear this special suit, which can easily be made as follows:

YOU WILL NEED: Red jersey fleece fabric (to find the amount of fabric needed simply lay pattern pieces on the floor within the same measurement as the width of the fabric); 5cm wide strips of Terylene wadding, plus a 35cm x 25cm rectangle of wadding; 2cm wide elastic to fit around waist and both legs; 50 cm of narrow cord elastic; red sewing thread; fabric glue; five press studs; one white bobble.

TO COMPLETE THE OUTFIT: Black boots; green mittens; black belt with gold buckle; sack.

TO MAKE: 1.5cm seams taken throughout, with fabric right sides together. Press each seam open after sewing.

1/ Turn under 1.5cm on front neck, sleeve cuffs, front and back jacket hems, and hood (between points C and A), and stitch 1cm in from fold.

2/ Join shoulder seams AB, then sew hood to back neck along line AA. Join seam CD on hood.

3/ Sew sleeves to jacket along line FBF.

4/ Join sleeve and side seams, EFG. Turn under 5cm down jacket fronts and stitch 4cm in from fold.

5/ Join inside leg seams, JK, on each trouser leg. Pin legs together and sew seam LJM round crutch.

6/ Turn under 4cm at waist and base of legs, and stitch 3cm in from fold, leaving a space open. Thread each hem with elastic, adjusting to fit. Join elastic and sew across openings.

7/ With fabric glue, attach strips of wadding to hood and jacket. Position and sew press studs to jacket fronts, overlapping front edges by 5cm. Sew bobble to point of hood.

8/ Sew elastic loops to sides of beard, adjusting to fit, and attach eyebrows to face with eyelash glue.

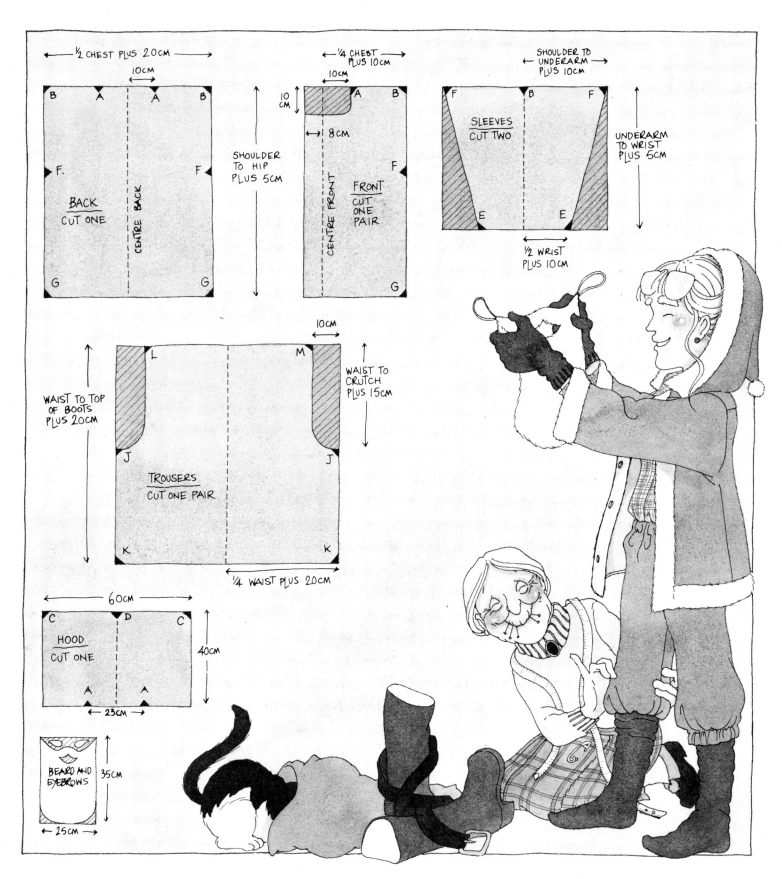

½ CHEST PLUS 20CM

10CM

B   A   A   B

F.   F

BACK
CUT ONE

CENTRE BACK

G   G

SHOULDER
TO HIP
PLUS 5CM

¼ CHEST
PLUS 10CM

10CM

10
CM

A   B

8CM

CENTRE FRONT

F

FRONT
CUT
ONE
PAIR

G

SHOULDER TO
UNDERARM
PLUS 10CM

F   B   F

SLEEVES
CUT TWO

E   E

½ WRIST
PLUS 10CM

UNDERARM
TO WRIST
PLUS 5CM

10CM

L   M

WAIST TO
CRUTCH
PLUS 15CM

J   J

WAIST TO TOP
OF BOOTS
PLUS 20CM

TROUSERS
CUT ONE PAIR

K   K

¼ WAIST PLUS 20CM

60CM

C   D   C

HOOD
CUT ONE

A   A

23CM

40CM

**BEARD AND
EYEBROWS**

35CM

25CM

Party Hats

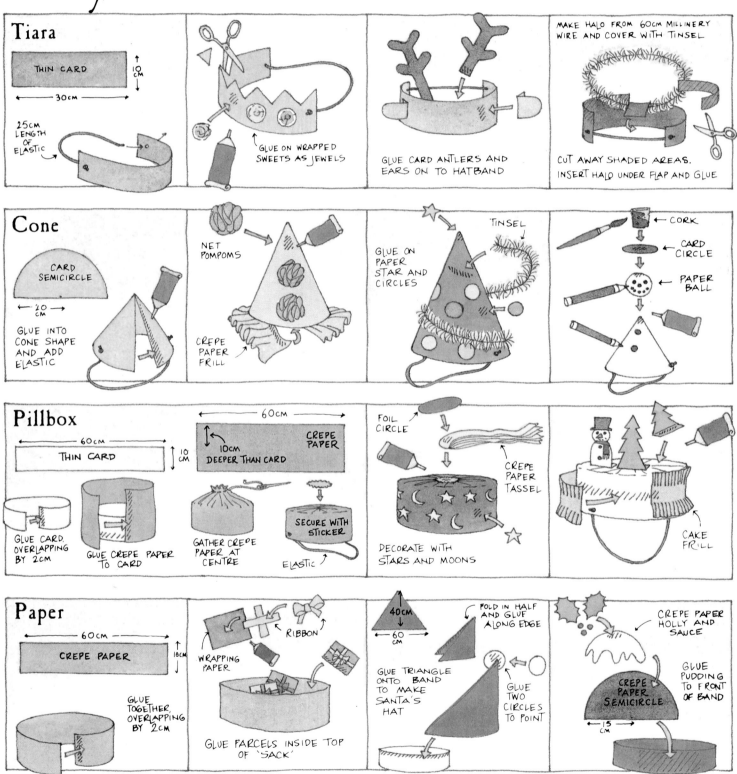

Tiara

THIN CARD — 30cm × 10cm

25cm LENGTH OF ELASTIC

GLUE ON WRAPPED SWEETS AS JEWELS

GLUE CARD ANTLERS AND EARS ON TO HATBAND

MAKE HALO FROM 60cm MILLINERY WIRE AND COVER WITH TINSEL

CUT AWAY SHADED AREAS. INSERT HALO UNDER FLAP AND GLUE

Cone

CARD SEMICIRCLE — 20 cm

GLUE INTO CONE SHAPE AND ADD ELASTIC

NET POMPOMS

CREPE PAPER FRILL

GLUE ON PAPER STAR AND CIRCLES

TINSEL

CORK

CARD CIRCLE

PAPER BALL

Pillbox

THIN CARD — 60cm × 10cm

CREPE PAPER — 60cm — 10cm DEEPER THAN CARD

GLUE CARD, OVERLAPPING BY 2CM

GLUE CREPE PAPER TO CARD

GATHER CREPE PAPER AT CENTRE

SECURE WITH STICKER

ELASTIC

FOIL CIRCLE

CREPE PAPER TASSEL

DECORATE WITH STARS AND MOONS

CAKE FRILL

Paper

CREPE PAPER — 60cm × 18cm

GLUE TOGETHER, OVERLAPPING BY 2CM

WRAPPING PAPER

RIBBON

GLUE PARCELS INSIDE TOP OF 'SACK'

40CM / 60 CM

FOLD IN HALF AND GLUE ALONG EDGE

GLUE TRIANGLE ONTO BAND TO MAKE SANTA'S HAT

GLUE TWO CIRCLES TO POINT

CREPE PAPER HOLLY AND SAUCE

CREPE PAPER SEMICIRCLE — 15 cm

GLUE PUDDING TO FRONT OF BAND

Christmas Sweaters

To knit

To sew

Christmas Sweaters (Instructions)

Transform your sweaters for Christmas Day by using some of the following ideas.

ABBREVIATIONS: K = knit; P = purl; st (s) = stitch (es); beg =beginning; M = main colour; C = contrast; inc = increase; dec = decrease; cont = continue; st-st = stocking stitch; g-st = garter stitch; tog = together; sl = slip; PSSO = pass slipped stitch over.

CRACKERS

YARN: Oddments of double knitting in bright colours and black. NEEDLES: a pair of 4mm. TENSION: 22 sts and 30 rows to 10cm square.

CRACKER: With M cast on 11 sts and cont in st-st beg with a K row.*Work 6 rows in M. Next row: Keeping yarn not in use at back of work, K 1M, [1C, 3M] twice, 1C, 1M. Next row: P 3C, [1M, 3C] twice. Work 8 rows in C. Next row: K 3C, [1M, 3C] twice. Next row: P 1M [1C, 3M] twice, 1C, 1M. Work 6 rows in M.* For "pulled" crackers, cast off and work another piece to match. For complete crackers, repeat from * to * once more and cast off.

TO MAKE UP: Darn in ends and press. Gather along centre of each stripe worked in C, draw up tightly and secure. Sew crackers to sweater and embroider "snap" lines on "pulled" crackers with a few stitches in black yarn.

CHRISTMAS TREE

YARN: Oddments of 4 ply lurex yarn in silver, gold, and mixed colours; a small amount of white 4 ply yarn.
NEEDLES: A pair of 3.25mm.
TENSION: 28 sts and 30 rows to 10cm square.
BAUBLES: With coloured lurex cast on 8 sts and cont in st-st, working random stripes of colour. Work 1 row. Cast on 3 sts at beg of next 2 rows. Cast on 2 sts at beg of next 4 rows. Inc 1 st at beg of next 4 rows.
Work 2 rows. Inc 1 st at beg of next 2 rows. Work 8 rows. Dec

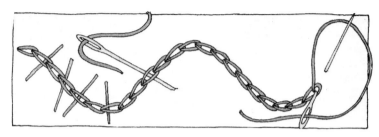

1 st at beg of next 2 rows. Work 2 rows. Dec 1 st at beg of next 4 rows. Cast off 2 sts at beg of next 4 rows. Cast off 3 sts at beg of next 2 rows. Work 1 row. Cast off.

CANDLES: With silver cast on 17 sts and cont in st-st. Work 2 rows. Cast off 4 sts at beg of next 2 rows [9 sts]. Work 6 rows. Change to white and work 26 rows. Cast off 3 sts at beg of next 2 rows [3 sts]. Change to gold and work 2 rows. Inc 1 st at beg of next 6 rows [9 sts.] Work 2 rows. Dec 1 st at beg and end of next 3 rows [3 sts]. Next row: P 3 tog, break yarn and draw through st.

TO MAKE UP: Darn in ends and press. Sew baubles and candles to sweater. To make "tinsel" embroider lines of chain stitch with silver, then work random stitches through chain.

SNOWMAN

YARN: One 20g ball of white mohair; oddments of double knitting in red, green and black. PLUS: black wooden beads. NEEDLES: A pair each of 5.5mm and 4mm. TENSION: 17 sts and 22 rows to 10cm square, with mohair on 5.5mm needles.
BODY: With 5.5mm needles and mohair cast on 22 sts and cont in st-st. Work 18 rows. Cast on 2 sts at beg of next 4 rows [30 sts]. Work 4 rows. Dec 1 st at beg of next 6 rows [24 sts]. Dec 1 st at beg and end of next 8 rows [8 sts]. Cast on 2 sts at beg of next 2 rows. Inc 1 st at beg of next 2 rows [14 sts]. Work 6 rows. Dec 1 st at beg of next 2 rows. Dec 1 st at beg and end of next 2 rows [8 sts]. Cast off.
HAT: With 4mm needles and black cast on 15 sts and work 18 rows st-st, cast off.

SCARF: With red cast on 9 sts and work 6 row g-st stripes of red and green until 54 rows have been worked, cast off. With red cast on 6 sts and work 6 row g-st stripes of red and green until 24 rows have been worked, cast off.

SNOWFLAKES: With 5.5mm needles and mohair make a loop and K into front and back of it three times [6 sts]. Rows 1, 2, 3, 4, & 5: Sl 1, K5. Row 6: [Sl 1, K 2 tog, PSSO] twice, pass first st over second, break yarn and draw through st.

TO MAKE UP: Darn in ends and press double knitting pieces. Sew snowman to sweater. Sew hat to head and embroider brim in black chain stitch. Sew short scarf piece across neck, and end of long scarf piece to top of neck. Sew snowflakes to sweater, and one to snowman's face for nose. Sew black beads to face for eyes and mouth.

SNOW CRYSTALS

MATERIALS: White yarn and a tapestry needle.
TO MAKE UP: Work four 5cm stitches to form a star shape. Where stitches cross secure to sweater with small stitches. Build up snow crystal patterns by working small V-shaped and straight stitches over star.

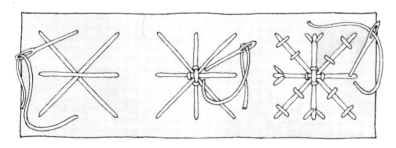

GIFT

MATERIALS: 4cm wide satin ribbon to fit round chest of sweater and from shoulder to top of rib on front and back, plus 60cm; a 10cm x 5cm rectangle of felt; embroidery cotton; matching sewing threads.
TO MAKE UP: Sew ribbon round chest, overlapping ends at left front. Sew ribbon from top of rib at front to top of rib at back, turning under 1cm at both ends. Make a bow from remaining ribbon and sew in place. Shape felt to form "tag" and sew in place. Embroider cord and message on tag with chain stitch.

STARRY NIGHT

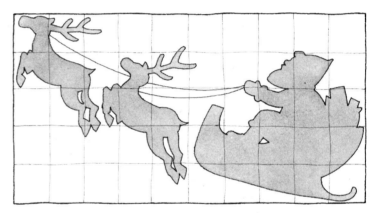

MATERIALS: 20cm x 10cm rectangle of black felt; black embroidery cotton; small silver star-shaped sequins; matching sewing threads.
TO MAKE UP: Following diagram, 1 square represents 2cm, cut silhouettes from felt and stitch to sweater. Embroider reins in chain stitch and sew on sequins.

SANTA

MATERIALS: 5cm wide strips of white fur fabric to fit round base of sweater, sleeve cuffs, and down front of sweater; 4cm wide black grosgrain ribbon to fit round sweater plus 10cm; 20cm of narrow gold braid; matching sewing threads.
TO MAKE UP: Sew fur fabric in place. Cut end of ribbon to a V and sew round waist, leaving end free. Sew gold braid to "belt" to make buckle.

Festive Jewellery

Necklaces

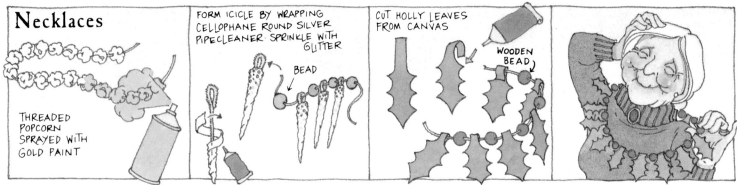

THREADED POPCORN SPRAYED WITH GOLD PAINT

FORM ICICLE BY WRAPPING CELLOPHANE ROUND SILVER PIPECLEANER. SPRINKLE WITH GLITTER

BEAD

CUT HOLLY LEAVES FROM CANVAS

WOODEN BEAD

Bracelets

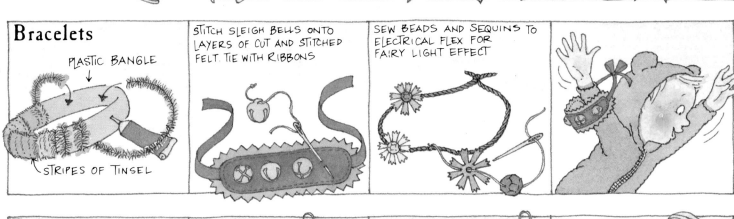

PLASTIC BANGLE

STRIPES OF TINSEL

STITCH SLEIGH BELLS ONTO LAYERS OF CUT AND STITCHED FELT. TIE WITH RIBBONS

SEW BEADS AND SEQUINS TO ELECTRICAL FLEX FOR FAIRY LIGHT EFFECT

Earrings

WRAPPING PAPER

EMPTY MATCHBOX

RIBBON

COVER CARD CIRCLE WITH TINSEL. GLUE ON RIBBON BOW

STITCHED FELT SOCK

RIBBON LOOP

Hair Trims

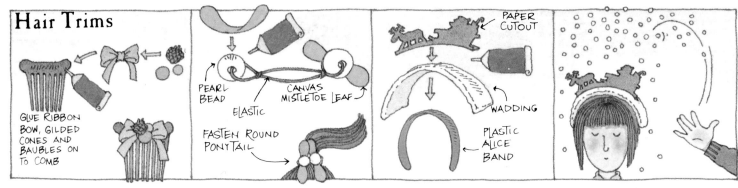

GLUE RIBBON BOW, GILDED CONES AND BAUBLES ON TO COMB

PEARL BEAD

ELASTIC

CANVAS MISTLETOE LEAF

FASTEN ROUND PONYTAIL

PAPER CUTOUT

WADDING

PLASTIC ALICE BAND

CHAPTER 5

Decorations and Wrapping

Making Wrapping Paper

Potato Cuts

PUSH A PASTRY CUTTER INTO CENTRE OF POTATO HALF—THEN SLICE AWAY 1CM AROUND SHAPE

SPREAD POSTER PAINT ONTO SAUCER...

...AND DIP POTATO INTO IT.

PRESS POTATO ONTO PAPER TO MAKE PATTERN...

...ALLOW TO DRY

Stencils

FOLD PAPER IN HALF, CUT OUT SHAPE ALONG FOLD, AND OPEN OUT.

PLACE STENCIL ON PAPER, AND DAB OVER MOTIF WITH SPONGE DIPPED IN PASTE

BEFORE PASTE DRIES, SPRINKLE GLITTER DUST OVER PAPER AND SHAKE OFF ANY EXCESS

Spray Paints

CUT SHAPES FROM THIN PAPER AND DAMPEN WITH A MOIST SPONGE

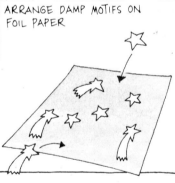

ARRANGE DAMP MOTIFS ON FOIL PAPER

SPRAY STRIPES ACROSS PAPER, USING DIFFERENT COLOURS OF SPRAY PAINTS...

...THEN PEEL OFF SHAPES

Marbling

MIX OIL PAINTS WITH TURPENTINE UNTIL RUNNY. POUR ONTO WATER IN STRIPES.

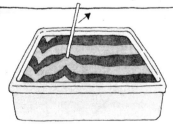

DRAW A STICK ACROSS THE LINES IN ALTERNATE DIRECTIONS.

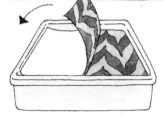

LAY A PIECE OF PAPER ON SURFACE OF WATER, PEEL OFF CAREFULLY AND ALLOW TO DRY

Bows and Trims

Star Bow

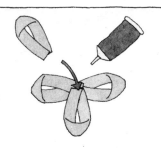

CUT SIXTEEN 12 CM LENGTHS OF RIBBON. TWIST AND GLUE AS SHOWN.

GLUE TOGETHER IN SETS OF FOUR TO FORM CROSSES.

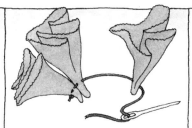

ASSEMBLE BY GLUEING TOGETHER-PLACING EACH CROSS DIAGONALLY ON TOP OF PREVIOUS CROSS. FINISH WITH LOOP.

Net Pompom

CUT EIGHT 10 CM CIRCLES OF NET

PINCH CENTRE OF EACH CIRCLE, CATCH TOGETHER WITH NEEDLE AND THREAD, AND SECURE.

BRUSH EDGES OF NET WITH PASTE AND SPRINKLE WITH GLITTER.

Patisserie

USING NARROW RIBBON, TIE ROUND PACKAGE.

LAY THREE 40 CM LENGTHS OF RIBBON ACROSS KNOT AND TIE A BOW

DRAW RIBBON ACROSS SCISSOR BLADE TO FORM RINGLETS

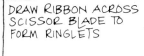

Looped Bow

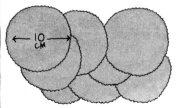

CUT SIX 25 CM LENGTHS OF RIBBON

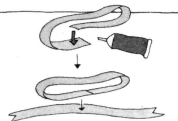

NOTCH BOTH ENDS OF ONE RIBBON, AND GLUE ENDS OF THE OTHERS TO FORM LOOPS. STACK ABOVE EACH OTHER

STAPLE THEM ALL TOGETHER AT CENTRE...

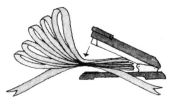

...AND GLUE BOW TO GIFT

Wrapping Awkward Shapes

Several Small Gifts

DRAW STOCKING SHAPE ON FOLDED FELT, AND SEW ALONG LINE

TRIM TO 1CM

PUNCH HOLES AND THREAD WITH RIBBON

To Anne with love from HENRY xx

Large and Ungainly

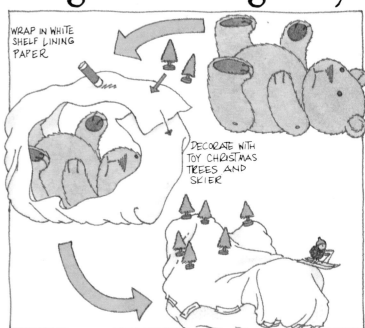

WRAP IN WHITE SHELF LINING PAPER

DECORATE WITH TOY CHRISTMAS TREES AND SKIER

Drum or Tin

WRAP WELL IN WHITE PAPER

GLUE ON CIRCLE OF WHITE CARD

GLUE ON CHOCOLATE TREE DECORATIONS AND TIE RIBBON

WRITE MESSAGE

MERRY CHRISTMAS

Bottle or Jar

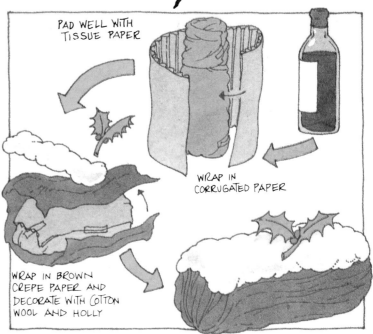

PAD WELL WITH TISSUE PAPER

WRAP IN CORRUGATED PAPER

WRAP IN BROWN CREPE PAPER AND DECORATE WITH COTTON WOOL AND HOLLY

Christmas Crackers

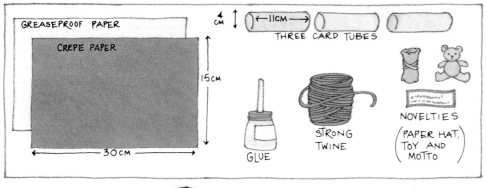

GREASEPROOF PAPER

CREPE PAPER

15CM

30CM

4 CM

←11CM→

THREE CARD TUBES

GLUE

STRONG TWINE

NOVELTIES
(PAPER HAT, TOY AND MOTTO)

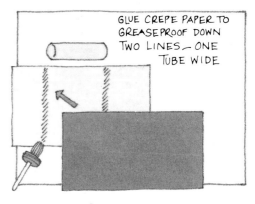

GLUE CREPE PAPER TO GREASEPROOF DOWN TWO LINES — ONE TUBE WIDE

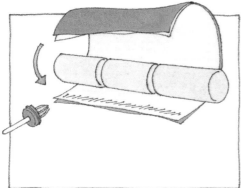

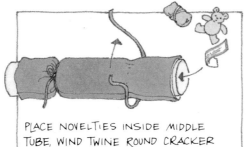

PLACE NOVELTIES INSIDE MIDDLE TUBE, WIND TWINE ROUND CRACKER WHERE TUBES MEET. PULL TIGHTLY AND KNOT

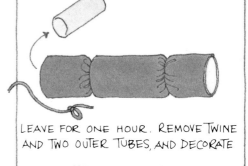

LEAVE FOR ONE HOUR. REMOVE TWINE AND TWO OUTER TUBES, AND DECORATE

SPOTTY PAPER

CUTOUT FIGURE

FRINGED ENDS

DOILIES

RIBBON BOW

PAPER INITIAL

PAINTED CONES

NET BOW

PINKED EDGES

SEQUINS

Wreaths, Swags and Logs
Cornucopia Wreath

BIND STRAW WITH RAFFIA TO FORM A SAUSAGE. JOIN INTO A RING AND SECURE WITH RAFFIA.

TAKE SMALL BUNCHES OF GREENERY AND BIND ON TO WREATH WITH GREEN STRING.

TIE A RIBBON BOW ROUND TOP, AND DECORATE WITH FRUIT, BOWS AND GILDED CONES AND NUTS — BY TWISTING OR PIERCING WITH FLORIST'S WIRE AND PUSHING INTO WREATH.

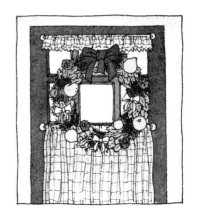

Greenery Swag

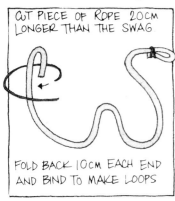

CUT PIECE OF ROPE 20CM LONGER THAN THE SWAG

FOLD BACK 10CM EACH END AND BIND TO MAKE LOOPS

BIND BUNCHES OF FOLIAGE TO ROPE WITH STRING, KEEPING BUNCHES LYING IN ONE DIRECTION

SLIP A CURTAIN RING ONTO RIBBON AND TIE A BOW AT EACH LOOPING POINT.

Yule Log

DRILL HOLES IN LOG TO HOLD CANDLES

MIX SOAP POWDER WITH WATER TO FORM A THICK PASTE AND WHIP UNTIL FROTHY

NAIL EVERGREENS TO LOG, THEN DECORATE WITH SOAP SNOW, AND BAUBLES

Garlands and Chains

Folded Fans

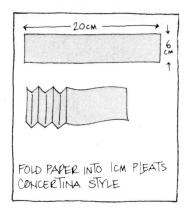

← 20cm →
↓ 6cm ↑

FOLD PAPER INTO 1CM PLEATS CONCERTINA STYLE

STAPLE ACROSS END OF FAN. REPEAT TO MAKE SEVERAL MORE.

GLUE EDGES OF FANS TOGETHER – ALTERNATING STAPLED ENDS.

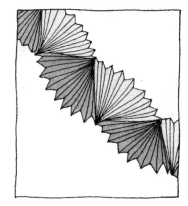

Twisting Spiral Chain

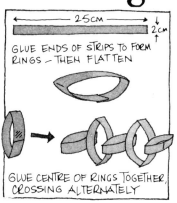

← 25cm →
↓ 2cm ↑

GLUE ENDS OF STRIPS TO FORM RINGS – THEN FLATTEN

GLUE CENTRE OF RINGS TOGETHER, CROSSING ALTERNATELY

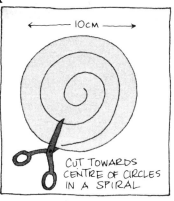

← 10cm →

CUT TOWARDS CENTRE OF CIRCLES IN A SPIRAL

THREAD SPIRAL TO EACH ALTERNATE RING, SECURING WITH A KNOT AT EACH END

Tissue Stars

← 10cm →

CUT TWO 6 POINTED STARS FROM CARD, AND A PILE OF STARS FROM FOLDED TISSUE PAPER

GLUE TISSUE STARS IN PAIRS AT THESE POINTS

WHEN DRY, GLUE PAIRS OF STARS TOGETHER AT THESE POINTS – THEN GLUE A CARD STAR AT EACH END OF GARLAND

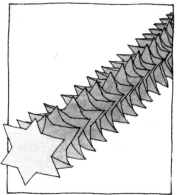

Peepshows

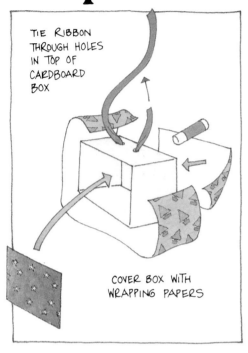

TIE RIBBON THROUGH HOLES IN TOP OF CARDBOARD BOX

COVER BOX WITH WRAPPING PAPERS

DECORATE AS YOU WISH (GLITTER, COTTON WOOL, ETC.)

CUT FIGURES FROM CHRISTMAS CARDS AND GLUE INSIDE BOX

Snow Scene

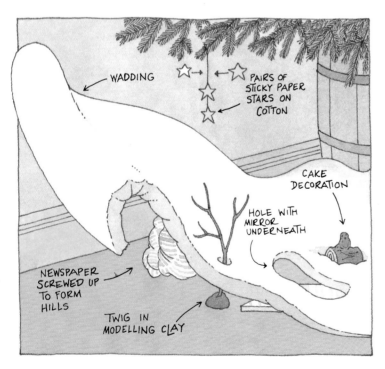

WADDING

PAIRS OF STICKY PAPER STARS ON COTTON

CAKE DECORATION

HOLE WITH MIRROR UNDERNEATH

NEWSPAPER SCREWED UP TO FORM HILLS

TWIG IN MODELLING CLAY

CHAPTER 6

The Christmas Tree

Types of Christmas Tree

Blocked Tree

Cut Tree

Imitation Tree

Rooted Tree

Looking After Christmas Trees

Any bare spaces can be filled by pushing spare branches, trimmed from base of tree, into holes drilled in trunk.

Blocked trees drop their needles quickly due to moisture loss. Spraying daily with lukewarm water helps to prevent this.

Soak the roots of bare rooted trees overnight in water, then pot the tree in moist soil. Place away from direct heat.

Cut 5cm from base of trunk and wedge in bucket or tub with stones and screwed-up newspapers. Keep container filled with water daily.

If space is limited, prune back of tree to a flat shape and place against a wall. Use cut branches to make wreaths and swags.

Victorian Tree

SUSPEND BIRD DECORATION BY NYLON THREAD STITCHED TO BACK

PIN RIBBON TO BEAK

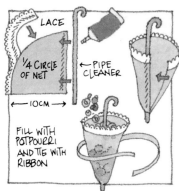

LACE

¼ CIRCLE OF NET

← PIPE CLEANER

10CM

FILL WITH POTPOURRI AND TIE WITH RIBBON

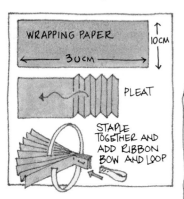

WRAPPING PAPER

10CM

30CM

PLEAT

STAPLE TOGETHER AND ADD RIBBON BOW AND LOOP

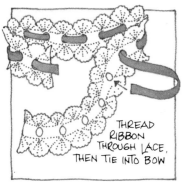

THREAD RIBBON THROUGH LACE, THEN TIE INTO BOW

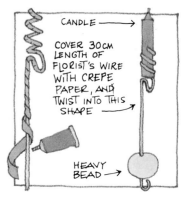

CANDLE →

COVER 30CM LENGTH OF FLORIST'S WIRE WITH CREPE PAPER, AND TWIST INTO THIS SHAPE →

HEAVY BEAD →

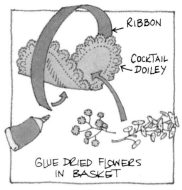

RIBBON

COCKTAIL DOILEY

GLUE DRIED FLOWERS IN BASKET

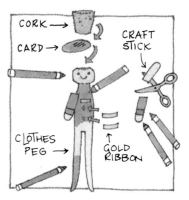

CORK →

CARD →

CRAFT STICK

CLOTHES PEG →

GOLD RIBBON

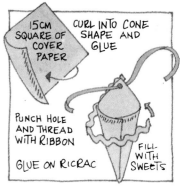

15CM SQUARE OF COVER PAPER

CURL INTO CONE SHAPE AND GLUE

PUNCH HOLE AND THREAD WITH RIBBON

GLUE ON RICRAC

FILL WITH SWEETS

Child's Own Tree

GLITTER

GLUE

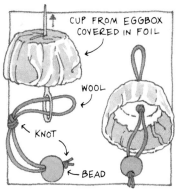

CUP FROM EGGBOX COVERED IN FOIL

WOOL

KNOT

BEAD

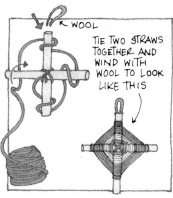

WOOL

TIE TWO STRAWS TOGETHER AND WIND WITH WOOL TO LOOK LIKE THIS

DOUGH = ONE CUP FLOUR AND ONE CUP SALT MIXED WITH WATER

ROLL OUT AND CUT INTO SHAPES

HOLE FOR RIBBON

HARDEN IN SLOW OVEN, THEN PAINT

WRAPPING PAPER

20 CM

10 CM

3 CM

RIBBON

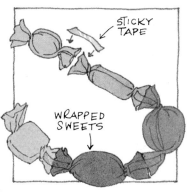

STICKY TAPE

WRAPPED SWEETS

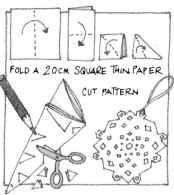

FOLD A 20CM SQUARE THIN PAPER

CUT PATTERN

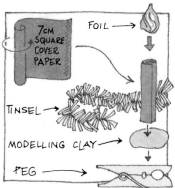

7CM SQUARE COVER PAPER

FOIL

TINSEL

MODELLING CLAY

PEG

Food Lover's Tree

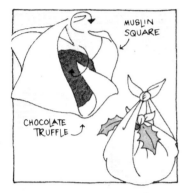

MUSLIN SQUARE

CHOCOLATE TRUFFLE

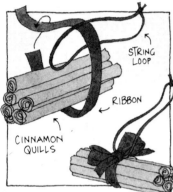

STRING LOOP

RIBBON

CINNAMON QUILLS

FORM INITIALS FROM BREAD DOUGH STRIPS

BRUSH WITH BEATEN EGG

SPRINKLE WITH SEEDS OR NUTS, AND BAKE

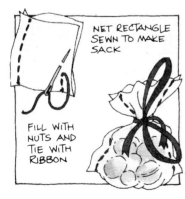

NET RECTANGLE SEWN TO MAKE SACK

FILL WITH NUTS AND TIE WITH RIBBON

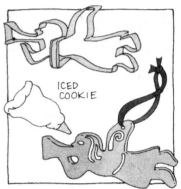

ICED COOKIE

POPPING CORN TO COVER BASE OF PAN

1 TABLESPOON HOT OIL

FILL CRACKER WITH FAVOURITE COFFEE BEANS

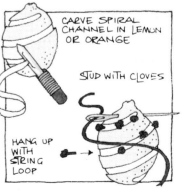

CARVE SPIRAL CHANNEL IN LEMON OR ORANGE

STUD WITH CLOVES

HANG UP WITH STRING LOOP

Wildlife Tree

PEANUT

ROSEHIP

STRING

CUT SHAPES FROM BREAD AND DRY IN SLOW OVEN

SPREAD FIRCONE WITH PEANUT BUTTER, AND DIP INTO BIRD SEED

MELTED FAT AND SEEDS

HOT SKEWER

LEAVE TO SET

STRING

BEAD

TIE SIX PIECES OF MILLET TOGETHER TO FORM STAR

SUNFLOWER SEEDS

APPLE

STRING

RIBBON

SWEETCORN

COCONUT

HOLE

STRING

BEAD

49

Soft and Safe Tree

STUFF WITH KAPOK

FELT

COTTON WOOL BALLS

RIBBON   FOAM STRIPS

BEND INTO HEART SHAPE AND GLUE

TWO CARD CIRCLES

WIND WITH COLOURED WOOLS TO COVER FOUR TIMES.

CUT, TIE AND NEATEN

RIBBONS

RIBBON

FELT ¼ CIRCLE

PAPER BALL

STRANDS OF WOOL TIED WITH PIPE CLEANERS

GLUE TOGETHER

FABRIC

FOAM CUBE

TIE GLUED PARCEL WITH WOOL

PAPER STAR

RIBBON

GATHERED NET SKIRT

CHAPTER 7

Father Christmas

Writing to Father Christmas

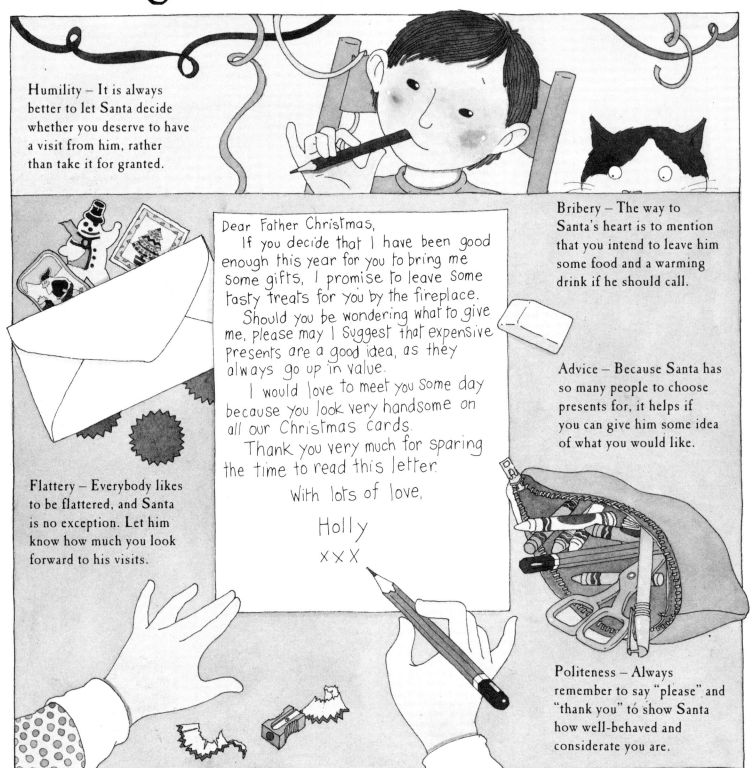

Humility – It is always better to let Santa decide whether you deserve to have a visit from him, rather than take it for granted.

Bribery – The way to Santa's heart is to mention that you intend to leave him some food and a warming drink if he should call.

Advice – Because Santa has so many people to choose presents for, it helps if you can give him some idea of what you would like.

Flattery – Everybody likes to be flattered, and Santa is no exception. Let him know how much you look forward to his visits.

Dear Father Christmas,
   If you decide that I have been good enough this year for you to bring me some gifts, I promise to leave some tasty treats for you by the fireplace.
   Should you be wondering what to give me, please may I suggest that expensive presents are a good idea, as they always go up in value.
   I would love to meet you some day because you look very handsome on all our Christmas cards.
   Thank you very much for sparing the time to read this letter.
        With lots of love,

           Holly
           x x x

Politeness – Always remember to say "please" and "thank you" to show Santa how well-behaved and considerate you are.

From Letter to Sack

After your letter to Father Christmas has been written and posted (or left somewhere to be collected), a lot happens before you receive your gifts. Here you can see how your request is taken to be processed in the elf workshops, making sure that the correct presents are placed in Santa's sack ready to be delivered to you.

Yule Lodge

Father Christmas lives in a quaint wooden house built high amongst the trees, which might even be in a forest near to your home. This is where all your letters are delivered, and where the elves spend many busy weeks leading up to Christmas making and wrapping presents in their workshops. Santa's reindeer have their stables attached to the house, and as Christmas approaches they are given extra helpings of moss and hay to make them strong enough to pull the gift-laden sleigh. Afterwards they all return here to have a well-earned rest.

54

Food to Leave for Santa

Barley sugar sweets for Santa to suck if he starts to feel airsick, and extra strong peppermints to keep him warm on a frosty night.

Decorate mince pies with stars cut from left-over pastry. Dust with icing sugar and pile on a plate with a chunk of cake.

Roll and cut bread dough into a tree shape and snip surface with scissors. Bake and serve with sharp cheese and crunchy pickles.

Don't forget the reindeer! Leave them a bundle of sweet meadow hay, a bunch of reindeer moss and a crisp red apple.

Leave a jug of hot cocoa with a sifter of chocolate and cinnamon, and a bowl of punch in case Santa feels like something stronger.

Chimneys

Although factory chimneys are the easiest to get in and out of, with the help of a rope, gifts are usually delivered to your home.

Mesh guards, to stop birds nesting, can prove to be difficult to remove and replace if Santa has forgotten his tool kit.

A cowl on a chimney-top is tricky to squeeze through, although it does stop snow falling onto Santa's head once he is in the chimney.

A wide-necked chimney-pot with a rounded edge is easy to get down, and good footholds can be found in brick or stone stacks.

A chimney-pot with a pointed edge is extremely uncomfortable to get down, and could catch Santa's beard or tear his clothes.

The Busiest Time of the Year

CHAPTER 8

Festive Fare

Figgy Pudding

MILK
DRIED FIGS
EGGS
BLACK TREACLE
BUTTER
BAKING POWDER
CINNAMON
GRATED NUTMEG
PLAIN FLOUR
BROWN SUGAR
ICING SUGAR
GRATED LEMON RIND
CREAM
HOLLY
FRESH WHITE BREADCRUMBS

IF YOU HAVEN'T MADE THE CHRISTMAS PUDDING BY STIR-UP SUNDAY (THE LAST SUNDAY BEFORE ADVENT) HERE'S A RECIPE FOR ONE THAT DOESN'T NEED TO MATURE.

CUT STEMS FROM 250G DRIED FIGS WITH KITCHEN SCISSORS, THEN CUT INTO SMALL PIECES. THIS IS VERY STICKY, SO BE WARNED!

SIMMER THE FIGS IN 200ML MILK FOR 25 MINUTES, REMOVE FROM HEAT AND STIR IN 1 TABLESPOON BLACK TREACLE

MIX TOGETHER IN BOWL: 150G FLOUR, 100G BROWN SUGAR, 50G BREADCRUMBS, 1 TEASPOON EACH OF BAKING POWDER, CINNAMON AND NUTMEG, AND THE GRATED RIND OF 1 LEMON. THEN ADD FIG MIXTURE, 100G MELTED BUTTER, AND 2 BEATEN EGGS. MIX WELL.

BUTTER A 1 LITRE PUDDING BASIN AND SPOON IN MIXTURE

COVER WITH LAYER OF GREASEPROOF PAPER AND ONE OF FOIL, AND TIE STEAM FOR TWO HOURS.

TURN OUT ONTO A PLATE, DUST WITH ICING SUGAR AND DECORATE WITH SPRIG OF HOLLY. SERVE WITH WHIPPED CREAM.

I DON'T NORMALLY GIVE THIS RECIPE AWAY, BUT YOU'RE SPECIAL!

Warming Punches

ALCOHOLIC PUNCH:-

ORANGES   CLOVES   GRATED NUTMEG

DEMERARA SUGAR

RED WINE   CINNAMON STICKS

CUT AN ORANGE INTO 4 PIECES AND PUSH 3 CLOVES INTO EACH PIECE

MIX TOGETHER 1 LITRE RED WINE (I'M USING A MIXTURE OF MY HOMEMADE ELDERBERRY AND BLACKBERRY), 200G SUGAR, AND ½ TEASPOON GRATED NUTMEG

POUR INTO A LARGE SAUCEPAN (DON'T USE ALUMINIUM OR ENAMEL AS THEY REACT WITH THE ALCOHOL — DON'T WE ALL!) WITH THE ORANGE PIECES AND GENTLY HEAT UNTIL ALMOST BOILING

STRAIN INTO A PUNCH BOWL AND FLOAT SLICES OF ORANGE ON TOP

SERVE IN MUGS WITH A CINNAMON STICK

NON - ALCOHOLIC PUNCH:-

AMERICAN GINGER ALE

UNSWEETENED APPLE JUICE   UNSWEETENED PINEAPPLE JUICE

CINNAMON

LEMON JUICE   APPLE   SUGAR CUBES

RUB 3 SUGAR CUBES OVER SURFACE OF A LEMON UNTIL THEY TURN YELLOW. MIX TOGETHER WITH 500ML APPLE JUICE, 500ML PINEAPPLE JUICE, 250ML GINGER ALE, 1 TEASPOON LEMON JUICE AND ½ TEASPOON CINNAMON. STIR UNTIL SUGAR IS DISSOLVED.

HEAT UNTIL ALMOST BOILING AND POUR INTO GLASSES DECORATED WITH APPLE SLICES.

Savoury Chestnut Log

DRIED CHESTNUTS, ONION, GARLIC, VEGETABLE STOCK CUBE, EGGS, MIXED HERBS, SALT, CELERY, PUFF PASTRY, BLACK PEPPER, COOKING OIL, PLAIN FLOUR, GROUND ALMONDS, CHESTNUT PUREE, BREADCRUMBS, WHITE WINE

SOAK 100G DRIED CHESTNUTS OVERNIGHT IN COLD WATER. SIMMER IN FRESH WATER FOR 30 MINUTES, DRAIN AND CHOP

SAUTÉ 1 CHOPPED ONION AND 2 CRUSHED CLOVES OF GARLIC IN 2 TABLESPOONS OIL UNTIL SOFT

STIR IN 2 TABLESPOONS FLOUR, THEN ADD 100ML WINE, 50ML WATER, AND CRUMBLED STOCK CUBE. STIR UNTIL THICK AND REMOVE FROM HEAT

STIR IN 2 BEATEN EGGS, 250G TINNED CHESTNUT PUREE, AND 50G DRY BREADCRUMBS

ADD 2 STICKS FINELY DICED CELERY, CHOPPED CHESTNUTS, 2 TEASPOONS MIXED HERBS, 1 TEASPOON SALT AND BLACK PEPPER TO TASTE — MMM!

ROLL AND TRIM 500G PUFF PASTRY TO 30CM SQUARE.

PLACE MIXTURE DOWN CENTRE OF PASTRY AND PINCH EDGES TOGETHER. CUT TRIMMINGS INTO THIN STRIPS, WIND INTO 2 SPIRALS AND FIT IN EACH END OF LOG.

PLACE ON GREASED BAKING TRAY, BRUSH WITH BEATEN EGG AND BAKE FOR 1 HOUR AT 375°F, 190°C, GAS MARK 5

SPRINKLE WITH GROUND ALMONDS AND ADD ROBIN DECORATION

Spiced Nuts

SAVOURY ALMONDS:—

COOKING OIL · SOY SAUCE · TABASCO · SALT · PAPRIKA · EGG · SESAME SEEDS · SHELLED ALMONDS

MIX TOGETHER 1 TABLESPOON EACH OF OIL, SOY SAUCE, AND SESAME SEEDS, 1 EGG WHITE AND A DASH OF TABASCO. ADD 125G SHELLED ALMONDS AND STIR UNTIL NUTS ARE COATED

SPREAD ON A BAKING SHEET AND BAKE AT 275°F, 140°C, GAS MARK 1 FOR 15 MINUTES, TURNING NUTS SO THEY ROAST EVENLY

MIX TOGETHER 1 TEASPOON EACH OF SALT AND PAPRIKA, AND ROLL NUTS IN MIXTURE WHILST STILL HOT. LEAVE TO COOL

SWEET WALNUTS:—

BROWN SUGAR · CORNFLOUR · CINNAMON · ALLSPICE · EGG · NUTMEG · WALNUTS

MIX TOGETHER 50G SUGAR, 20G CORNFLOUR, 1½ TEASPOONS CINNAMON, AND ½ TEASPOON EACH OF ALLSPICE AND NUTMEG

BEAT TOGETHER 1 EGG WHITE AND 1 TABLESPOON WATER. TIP 125G WALNUTS INTO EGG MIXTURE AND STIR TO COAT

DROP WALNUTS SINGLY INTO DRY INGREDIENTS, TURN UNTIL COVERED THEN PLACE ON GREASED BAKING TRAY

BAKE FOR 1 HOUR AT 275°F, 140°C, GAS MARK 1, TURNING ONCE DURING COOKING. LEAVE TO COOL. THEY'RE GREAT TO NIBBLE DURING CHRISTMAS!

Christmas Pudding Truffles

BUTTER

ICING SUGAR

VANILLA ESSENCE

CHOCOLATE SUGAR STRANDS

COCOA

ARTIFICIAL HOLLY

DOUBLE CREAM

CAKE

IN A BOWL, CREAM TOGETHER 50G BUTTER, 125G ICING SUGAR, 2 TABLESPOONS COCOA...

...2 TABLESPOONS DOUBLE CREAM, AND ½ TEASPOON VANILLA ESSENCE — EXCUSE ME WHILE I JUST CONCENTRATE

ADD 250G CAKE CRUMBS AND MIX WELL—WE CAN HAVE THE REST OF THE CAKE FOR TEA

ROLL INTO BALLS ABOUT THE SIZE OF A WALNUT—I HAPPEN TO HAVE ONE HERE TO HELP YOU

ROLL EACH BALL IN CHOCOLATE SUGAR STRANDS TO COVER—I LIKE TO KEEP A STORE OF THESE AS I HAVE A SWEET TOOTH

MIX 50G ICING SUGAR WITH 1 TEASPOON HOT WATER AND DROP A SMALL AMOUNT ONTO THE TOP OF EACH TRUFFLE—THIS NEEDS A STEADY HAND!

DECORATE WITH TINY SPRIGS OF ARTIFICIAL HOLLY

THIS ACTUALLY MAKES 16 TRUFFLES, BUT AS THERE ARE 7 IN OUR FAMILY, IT SAVES ARGUMENTS IF I EAT 2 NOW —THEN IT'S JUST 2 EACH!

Cream Cheese Snowmen

WHITE BREADCRUMBS

CHOPPED MIXED NUTS

CREAM CHEESE

DESSICATED COCONUT

CARROTS

SALT

COCKTAIL STICKS

MEASURE 100G FRESH WHITE BREADCRUMBS, 100G CHOPPED MIXED NUTS, AND 250G CREAM CHEESE INTO A BOWL TOGETHER WITH A PINCH OF SALT AND MIX WELL

DIVIDE MIXTURE INTO 2 PIECES, ONE TWICE THE SIZE OF THE OTHER, AND ROLL 12 BALLS FROM EACH PORTION

ROLL EACH BALL IN DESSICATED COCONUT TO COVER—THIS IS A BIT MESSY

MAKE HAT FROM PEELED CARROT BY CUTTING A 1.5CM LENGTH FROM POINTED END, AND A THIN SLICE FROM THE THICK END

I'M ALLOWED TO USE A KNIFE IF AN ADULT WATCHES ME — SO YOU BE CAREFUL TOO!

PUSH A COCKTAIL STICK THROUGH CARROT PIECES, THEN THROUGH HEAD AND BODY OF SNOWMAN

MARK EYES, MOUTH AND BUTTONS WITH A COCKTAIL STICK...

...AND INSERT A SLIVER OF CARROT FOR NOSE

THIS MAKES 12 SNOWMEN AND THEY'RE REALLY TASTY!

Chocolates and Candies

CHOCOLATE CREAMS :-

ICING SUGAR

EGG

PLAIN CHOCOLATE

FLAVOURING ESSENCES

FOOD COLOURING

MIX TOGETHER 250G ICING SUGAR AND 1 LIGHTLY BEATEN EGG WHITE AND KNEAD UNTIL SMOOTH

DIVIDE INTO 3 PORTIONS THEN ADD A FEW DROPS OF COLOURING AND FLAVOURING TO EACH PIECE AND KNEAD UNTIL EVENLY COLOURED

VIOLET ESSENCE + MAUVE COLOUR =

ROSE ESSENCE + PINK COLOUR =

PEPPERMINT ESSENCE + GREEN COLOUR =

ROLL EACH PIECE TO 6MM THICK, CUT INTO SHAPES, PLACE ON FOIL AND LEAVE TO DRY OVERNIGHT

MELT 200G CHOCOLATE AND DIP IN EACH SWEET TO COAT HALF LEAVE ON FOIL TO SET

WITH THE REMAINING CHOCOLATE I'LL MAKE SOME NUT CLUSTERS - MIX 175G MIXED NUTS AND 50G RAISINS WITH THE CHOCOLATE. DROP SMALL SPOONFULS ONTO FOIL AND LEAVE TO SET

STUFFED DATES :-

MARZIPAN

DATES

CASTER SUGAR

DIVIDE A 125G BLOCK OF MARZIPAN INTO 20 PIECES AND ROLL EACH INTO A SAUSAGE SHAPE

REMOVE STONES FROM 20 DATES, PLACE MARZIPAN INSIDE EACH DATE AND ROLL IN CASTER SUGAR

CHAPTER 9

Christmas Fun and Games

Charades

The game of charades involves one person acting out the name of a song, television programme, book, film or play without making any sound, whilst the other people try to guess the mime. Begin by holding up the same number of fingers as there are words, then mime the words in turn. The actions shown below will be of some help.

SONG: Open mouth and arms, as in singing.

TELEVISION: Draw square shape in front of you.

BOOK: Open hands like the pages of a book.

FILM: Pretend to wind an old movie camera.

PLAY: Draw two curves like opening curtains.

THE WHOLE THING: Draw a circle in front of you.

SOUNDS LIKE: Tug your ear lobe.

SIMILAR: Rock clenched hands to and fro.

SHORTER OR LONGER: Move hands closer or apart.

SMALL WORD: Pretend to hold tiny word.

PROPER NAME: Pat top of head with hand.

SYLLABLES: On upper arm indicate with fingers.

Charades can be played in three ways. 1. The first player thinks up a mime, and the one who guesses it correctly takes over. 2. Two teams choose their own subjects, and a member from one team mimes to the other team in turn. 3. The titles are written on pieces of paper by someone who is not playing, and are drawn in turn from a hat.

Pass the Present

With paper taken from the Christmas presents, wrap a small gift to make a large parcel. One person whistles, the players sit in a circle, and the parcel is passed round clockwise. When the music stops, the person holding the parcel begins to open it, but must pass it on as the music starts. The winner is the one who unwraps the gift.

Build a Snowman

The object of this game is to be the first person to complete a drawing of a snowman by throwing a die. The correct number must be thrown before each part of the snowman can be drawn in this order: body (6); head (5); hat (4); scarf (3); three buttons (2 for each); eyes, then nose, and then mouth (1 for each).

Pin the Star on the Tree

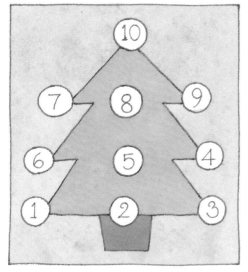

Copy the Christmas tree shown in the diagram onto a large sheet of paper, and pin to a wall. Cut a star from gold paper and push a drawing pin through it. Blindfold one player, turn them round three times, then ask them to pin the star on top of the tree. Count up everybody's scores, and the highest number wins.

Popcorn Chain

Divide players into two teams, get them to stand in line, and give each person a drinking straw. Place a bowl of popcorn at one end of each line, and an empty bowl at the other end. The object is to get the most pieces of popcorn into the empty bowls in 2 minutes, passing it between players by sucking it up with the straws.

Snowball!

Two teams of players sit at a table and a cotton wool ball is given to one team. These players pass the ball between them, under the table, then place their fists on the table. A member of the other team guesses which hand holds the ball and touches it, shouting "SNOWBALL!". The ball is passed to that team if the guess is correct.

Blow out the Candles

Cut 1cm tabs round the base of a card tube and bend outwards. Glue to an 8cm circle of card and glue a card flame to top of tube. Make nine more candles and paint. Place in the formation shown, and stand 3 metres away. Take turns to roll a soft ball at the candles, and keep a score of how many you knock over. The highest number wins.

Fill Santa's Sack

Open a large brown paper bag and place on the floor. Divide a pack of coloured cotton wool balls into even groups of pink, yellow, blue and white. Four players choose a colour each,

stand with their backs 2 metres from the bag, and throw the balls over their shoulders. Count the number of balls each player gets into Santa's sack.

Musical Crackers

On a table place one less cracker than there are players. When the music starts the players walk clockwise round the table, and as the music stops everyone grabs a cracker. The person

without one drops out of the game, and one cracker is removed. Continue until one cracker remains, which is given to the player holding it.

Christmas Tree Lights Game

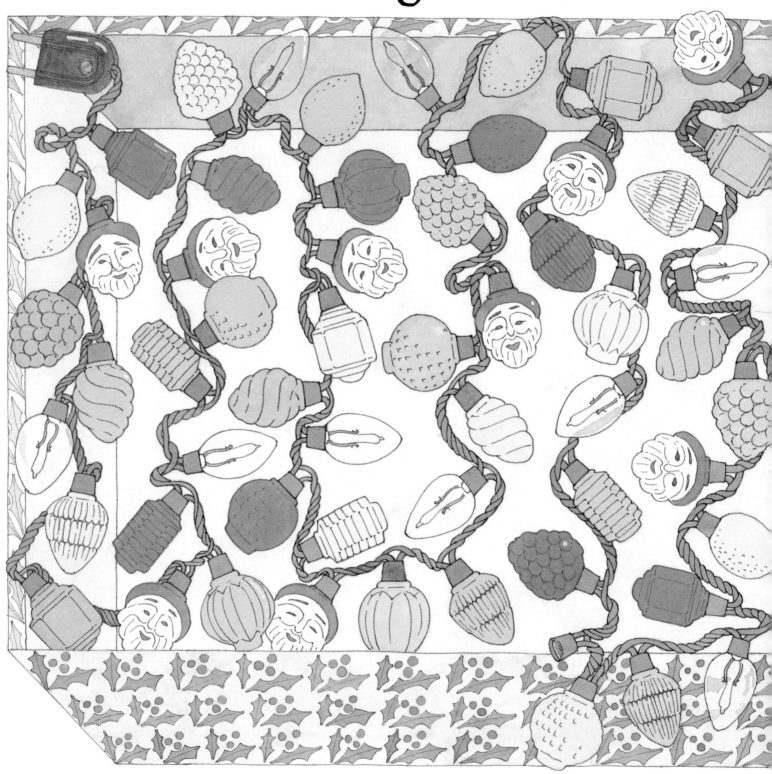

Up to four players choose a colour each. Start at the plug, and move counters along the lights by throwing a die. If you land on a Santa bulb, go on to the next bulb in your colour. If you land on a clear bulb, go back to the last bulb in your colour. Landing on an empty socket sends you back to the start. First to reach the star wins.

Puzzles and Tricks
Sleeping Snowbaby

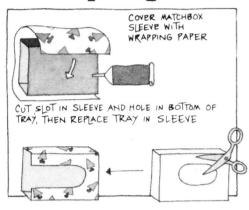

COVER MATCHBOX SLEEVE WITH WRAPPING PAPER

CUT SLOT IN SLEEVE AND HOLE IN BOTTOM OF TRAY, THEN REPLACE TRAY IN SLEEVE

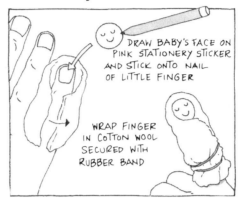

DRAW BABY'S FACE ON PINK STATIONERY STICKER AND STICK ONTO NAIL OF LITTLE FINGER

WRAP FINGER IN COTTON WOOL SECURED WITH RUBBER BAND

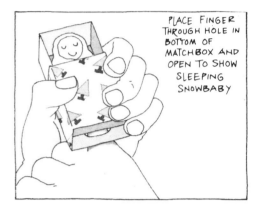

PLACE FINGER THROUGH HOLE IN BOTTOM OF MATCHBOX AND OPEN TO SHOW SLEEPING SNOWBABY

Spinning Medallion

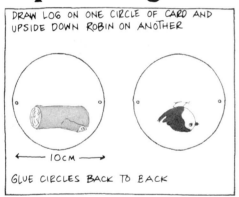

DRAW LOG ON ONE CIRCLE OF CARD AND UPSIDE DOWN ROBIN ON ANOTHER

← 10CM →

GLUE CIRCLES BACK TO BACK

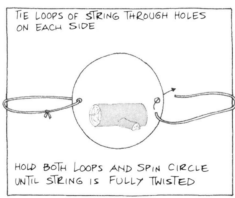

TIE LOOPS OF STRING THROUGH HOLES ON EACH SIDE

HOLD BOTH LOOPS AND SPIN CIRCLE UNTIL STRING IS FULLY TWISTED

AS CIRCLE SPINS, THE ROBIN WILL APPEAR TO BE STANDING ON LOG

Mirror Drawing

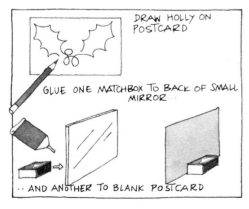

DRAW HOLLY ON POSTCARD

GLUE ONE MATCHBOX TO BACK OF SMALL MIRROR...

...AND ANOTHER TO BLANK POSTCARD

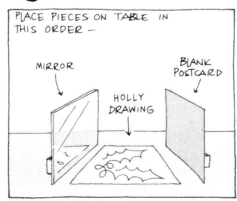

PLACE PIECES ON TABLE IN THIS ORDER —

MIRROR

HOLLY DRAWING

BLANK POSTCARD

TRY TO TRACE ROUND HOLLY WHILST LOOKING IN MIRROR

Gnome Visitor

Go Back, Rudolph!

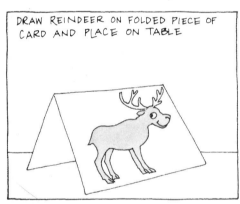

Tie the Parcel

Rescue Baby!

Here is a game for one player. You have to rescue Baby, who has become entangled with paperchains. First throw a die to see which member of the family is going to help you, and start at the number you have thrown. Follow the chain carefully to try and reach Baby in the middle, then return along the chain to your starting point.

CHAPTER 10
After Christmas

Keeping in Touch

The lull after Christmas, and before the celebrations of New Year, is ideal for writing to, or telephoning, friends and relations to thank for gifts – and also an opportunity to renew old friendships. Many people visit relatives who were unable to join them for the holidays, maybe taking some left-over treats to share.

"Thank You"

Visiting Relatives

New Year

Just before midnight on 31st December the front door and windows are opened to let out the old year and let in the new. To bring luck to the house someone tall and dark should "First Foot", carrying salt for food, coal for heat, and a coin for wealth. People also make resolutions to improve themselves in the coming year.

First Footing

Resolutions

It's Better to Give . . .

CHAPTER 11

Christmas Around the World

Sweden

In Sweden the celebrations last for a month – from Saint Lucia's Day on 13th December to Saint Knut's Day on 13th January. On Saint Lucia's Day, Swedish families are awakened with coffee and freshly baked buns by the daughter of the house. She is dressed in a white gown with a red sash, and wears on her head a wreath of greenery topped with lighted candles. Often she is joined by "Star Boys", who wear pointed hats, and carry star wands. To end the Christmas meal "rice porridge" is served. This is rice pudding containing a single almond . . . the person who finds the nut will marry within the next year!

Denmark

A traditional Danish Christmas tree decoration is a woven, heart-shaped paper basket, which is filled with sweets. Other decorations are made from carved wood, woven and plaited straw, and coloured paper. The tree is topped with a shining star, and lit by candles. Each Sunday in Advent, guests are invited to join in the lighting of the candles on the Advent crown. Adults drink a warming mixture of red wine, spices and raisins, and children drink a sweet fruit juice, such as strawberry. Everybody eats small cakes of batter which have been cooked over the fire in a special pan, and dusted with icing sugar.

Finland

In Finland everybody's house is given a thorough cleaning in readiness for Christmas. In the kitchen, hours are spent cooking and baking special treats for the festive season. Before Christmas Eve many people make a traditional visit to the famous Finnish steam baths. Fir trees are felled, tied onto sleds, and taken home to be decorated. Often a sheaf of grain is tied to a pole, together with nuts and seeds, and placed outside in the garden as a Christmas treat for the birds. It is said that many peasants will refuse to eat their Christmas meal until their feathered friends have been fed.

Norway

Norwegian children always remember a little gnome called "Nisse" at Christmastime. He guards all the farm animals, and he plays tricks on the children if they forget to put out a bowl of special porridge for him. A favourite holiday cookie called "sand kager" is made by mixing together 2 cups each of butter and sugar, 4 cups of flour, and 1 cup of chopped almonds. This is pressed into a tin, baked until golden brown, and cut into squares. In the dark afternoons the Viking tradition of "Christmas buck" is practised by children, dressed in outlandish outfits, who go from house to house asking for goodies.

Germany

In Germany Christmas preparations begin on the eve of 6th December. People often set aside special evenings for baking spiced cakes and cookies, and making gifts and decorations. Little dolls of fruit are traditional Christmas toys. They are easily made by forming a figure from plastic covered wire and threading with raisins, apple slices, and nuts. Children leave letters on their window sills for Christkind, a winged figure dressed in white robes and a golden crown, who distributes gifts. Sometimes these letters are decorated with glue and sprinkled with sugar to make them sparkle.

Austria

The feast of Saint Nicholas marks the beginning of Christmas in Austria. The saint, accompanied by the devil, asks children for a list of their good and bad deeds. Good children are given sweets, toys and nuts. Gifts, which have been placed under the tree, are opened after dinner on Christmas Eve. Austrian wax tree decorations can be made by pouring melted beeswax into patty pans or chocolate moulds, pushing a yarn loop into the wax, and leaving them to set. Brass instruments play chorale music from church steeples, and carol singers, carrying blazing torches and a manger from house to house, gather on the church steps.

Switzerland

As Christmas approaches, Swiss children eagerly await the tinkling of a silver bell that heralds the arrival of Christkindli – a white clad angel, with a face veil held in place by a jewelled crown. The tree candles are lit as she enters each house and hands out presents from the basket held by her child helpers. The week before Christmas children dress up and visit homes for small gifts. Bell ringing has become a tradition, and each village competes with the next when calling people to midnight mass. After the service, families gather to share huge homemade doughnuts called "ringli" and hot chocolate.

France

In France, on Christmas Eve, children leave their shoes by the fireplace to be filled with gifts by Père Noël. In the morning they also find that sweets, fruit, nuts and small toys have been hung on the tree. In cathedral squares the story of Christ's birth is re-enacted by both players and puppets. In addition to the usual Biblical characters, many cribs include painted clay figures called "santons", which represent people of everyday life, such as the priest, mayor, policeman, baker or grocer. These can be made from modelling clay, painted when hard, and added to your own crib.

Italy

The Italian festive season starts eight days before Christmas, and continues until Epiphany. A strict fast is observed for twenty-four hours before Christmas Eve, and is followed by a celebration meal, in which a light Milanese cake called "panettone" features. Presents, and sometimes empty boxes, are drawn from the "Urn of Fate" – a lucky dip, which always contains one gift per person. By twilight, candles are lighted around the family crib, prayers are said, and children recite poems. Befana, a kindly witch, arrives on 6th January and leaves gifts for good children, and a piece of charcoal for bad ones.

Spain

In Spain the Christmas festivities begin on 8th December, the Feast of the Immaculate Conception, when the Dance of the Sixes is performed. As in cathedrals and churches, most homes have a manger scene, complete with carved figures. During the week before Christmas, families gather round their manger to sing, whilst children play tambourines and dance. Shoes are placed on balconies on the night of 6th January, in the hope that the Wise Men will fill them with gifts. Often bundles of straw are also left for the camels. You could place a large foil star in your window to attract the Wise Men.

Australia

Christmas comes in the middle of the Australian summer, when the weather is very hot. After exchanging gifts at the breakfast table, many people have their Christmas Day meal on the beach, followed by a celebration supper. Homes are decorated with ferns and palm leaves, together with special flowers. One, called the Christmas bush, consists of hazy clusters of tiny flowers; another, the Christmas bell, is a bell-shaped flower with a yellow edge. A potted palm could be decorated to become a Christmas tree. As evening falls, parks fill with hundreds of people for carol services by candlelight.

Mexico

The Mexican home must be decorated, and ready to receive guests, by 16th December – the beginning of "Posadas", which commemorates Mary and Joseph's search for lodgings. Homes are festooned with Spanish moss, evergreens, and coloured lanterns and a crib is erected in the corner of one room. After prayers, fireworks are lit, and people gather to break the "Pinata" – an earthenware jar, filled with treats which is hung from the ceiling. Blindfolded children try to break it with a stick to release the contents. Simple pinatas can be easily made by covering inflated balloons with papier mâché.

United States

Christmas celebrations vary greatly between regions of the United States, as the inhabitants are of many ethnic origins. In Pennsylvania, the Moravians build a landscape – called a "putz" – under the Christmas tree; whilst the Germans are given gifts by Belsnickle, who taps them with his switch if they have misbehaved. In the South, firearms are shot to greet distant neighbours on Christmas Day. In Alaska a star on a pole is taken from door to door, followed by "Herod's men", who try to capture the star. Colonial doorways are often decorated with a pineapple, a symbol of hospitality.

Canada

Christmas is observed in Canada in very much the same manner as in northern parts of the United States – but also in other ways in some of its provinces: a big midwinter festival – called Sinck tuck, is celebrated by the Eskimos, with dancing and a present-giving party; in Labrador, turnips are saved from the summer harvest and are given to children, with a lighted candle pushed into a hollowed-out hole; and in Nova Scotia, a country settled by Scottish highlanders, songs and carols, brought from Brittany and the Basque country two centuries ago, are sung each Christmas morning.

CHAPTER 12

Twelfth Night

Taking Down Decorations

Twelfth Night, or Epiphany, falls on the 6th January, and marks the end of the Christmas holidays. After this date it is considered unlucky to still have decorations in the house, so we take them down, to be packed away safely until next Christmas. Greenery is taken outside and either planted in the garden or thrown away.

Half fill a jar with pine needles, add 1 teaspoon of vodka, and top up with corn oil. Shake daily for 1 week, strain and use as bath oil.

Iron large pieces of undamaged used wrapping paper and roll round a cardboard tube. Keep to wrap next year's gifts.

Small glass baubles can be packed in egg cartons. Larger decorations should be wrapped in tissue and packed between foam.

Tighten light bulbs, and wrap flex round a piece of card. Pack in a box, with a layer of cotton wool on each side for protection.

Greeting cards can be made into gift tags by cutting into rectangles, circles or triangles with pinking shears and adding yarn ties.

Useful Tips About Greenery

Keep a small piece of holly until next Christmas for good luck. Burn all other dead greenery, and use the ashes as a garden fertiliser.

Sprays of ivy, arranged in water with cut flowers, may have grown small roots by now. These can be planted outside to climb up a wall.

Remove dead greenery from the wreath. If the frame is metal, rub with wire wool and a little oil to prevent rusting, and pack away.

If your Christmas tree has roots, dig a hole in the garden, fork in some peat and firm the soil round the tree's roots. Water well.

With a knife, cut small flaps of bark underneath the branch of a tree and plant mistletoe berries by pressing under each flap.

A Christmas Collage

An unusual way to remember a special Christmas is to make a collage, using photographs, scraps of wrapping paper, gift tags, greeting cards, feathers and nuts gathered on walks, cracker scraps, paper hats, and pretty wrappers from sweets and chocolates eaten over the holidays. Every collage will be unique – just like every Christmas.

Index

Advent Calendars 13
Advent Crowns 12
After Christmas 79
Alaska 90
Alcoholic Punch 61
Angels in the Snow 25
Australia 89
Australian Christmas Bell 89
Australian Christmas Bush 89
Austria 86
Austrian Wax Decorations 86

Befana 88
Belsnickle 90
Blocked Tree 44
Blow out the Candles 72
Bobble Robin 20
Book Stand 17
Bottle or Jar, to wrap 38
Bow Ties 18
Bows and Trims 37
Bracelets 34
Build a Snowman 70

Canada 90
Candle Wreath 12
Carol Singing 25
Charades 68-69
Cheese Dish 19
Child's Own Tree 47
Chimneys 57
Chocolate Creams 66
Chocolate and Candies 66
Choosing Presents 22
Christkind 86
Christkindli 87
Christmas Around the World 83
Christmas Buck 85
Christmas Cards 14-15
Christmas Collage 94
Christmas Cracker card 15

Christmas Fun and Games 67
Christmas Pudding Truffles 64
Christmas Sweaters 31
Christmas Tree Lights Game 74-75
Christmas Tree sweater 32
Cone hat 30
Contents 5
Cookie Tree 13
Cornucopia Wreath 40
Countdown to Christmas 11
Crackers sweater 32
Crackers, to make 39
Cream Cheese Snowmen 65
Cut Tree 44

Dance of the Sixes 88
Decorations and Wrapping 35
Denmark 84
Drawer Scenter 21
Drum or Tin, to wrap 38

Earrings 34
Epiphany 92
Eskimos 90
Evergreens 26

Father Christmas 51
Father Christmas Outfit 28
Festive Fare 59
Festive Jewellery 34
Figgy Pudding 60
Fill Santa's Sack 73
Finland 85
Finnish Steam Baths 85
First Footing 81
Folded Fans 41
Food to Leave for Santa 56
Foodlover's Tree 48
France 87
From Letter to Sack 53

Garlands and Chains 41
German Fruit Dolls 86
Germany 86
Gift sweater 33
Gift tags, from cards 92
Glass decorations, to pack 92
Glitter Stars 12
Glove Puppets 16
Gnome Visitor 77
Go Back, Rudolph! 77
Greenery Swag 40

Hair Trims 34
Handmade Gifts 16-21
"Herod's Men" 90
Holly, in folklore 26
Holly, saving for luck 93

Imitation Tree 44
Immaculate Conception, feast 88
It's Better to Give . . . 82
Italy 88
Ivy, in folklore 26
Ivy, to plant 93

Keeping in Touch 80

Labrador 90
Large Gift, to wrap 38
Looking After Christmas Trees 45
Looped Bow 37

Marbling, on paper 36
Mirror Drawing 76
Mistletoe, in folklore 26
Mistletoe, to plant 93
Moravians 90
Musical Crackers 73

Necklaces 34
Net Pompom 37

New Year 81
Nisse 85
Non-alcoholic Punch 61
Norway 85
Nova Scotia 90
Nut Clusters 66

Origami Father Christmas card 14
Outside in the Snow 23

Palm Christmas Tree 89
Panettone 88
Paper hat 30
Party Hats 30
Pass the Present 70
Patisserie bow 37
Peepshows 42
Pennsylvania 90
Pennsylvanian Germans 90
Père Noel 87
Perfumed Treats 21
Pillbox hat 30
Pin the Star on the Tree 71
Pine needle oil 92
Pineapple, for hospitality 90
Pomander 21
Popcorn Chain 71
Potato Cuts, on paper 36
Putz 90
Puzzle Blocks 13
Puzzles and Tricks 76

Rescue Baby! 78
Resolutions 81
Rice porridge 84
Ringli 87
Rooted Tree 44
Rooted tree, to plant 93
Rosemary, in folklore 26

Saint Knut 84

Saint Lucia 84
Saint Nicholas 86
Sand Kager 85
Santa sweater 33
Santons 87
Savoury Almonds 63
Savoury Chestnut Log 62
Simmering Spice Sack 21
Sinck tuck 90
Sleeping Snowbaby 76
Small Gifts, to wrap 38
Snow Crystals sweater 33
Snow Scene 42
Snowball! 72
Snowcastles 24
Snowman sweater 32
Soft and Safe Tree 50
South, in United States 90
Spain 88
Spiced Nuts 63
Spinning Medallion 76
Spray Paints, on paper 36
Stained Glass Window card 14
Star Bow 37
Star Boys 84
Starry Night sweater 33
Stencils, on paper 36
Stuffed Dates 66
Sweater Instructions 32
Sweden 84
Sweet Walnuts 63
Switzerland 87

Taking Down Decorations 92
"Thank You" 80
The Busiest Time of the Year 58
The Christmas Tree 43
Tiara hat 30
Tie the Parcel 77
Tinsel Dome 12
Tinsel Family Tree 2

Tissue Paper Tree card 15
Tissue Stars 41
Treat Tree 13
Tree lights, to pack 92
Turnip and candle 90
Twelfth Night 91
Twisting Spiral Chain 41
Types of Christmas Tree 44

United States 90
Urn of Fate 88
Useful Tips About Greenery 93

Victorian Tree 46
Visiting Relatives 80

Warming Punches 61
What is Christmas? 7
Wildlife Tree 49
Wise Men 88
Woven heart basket 84
Wrapping Awkward Shapes 38
Wrapping paper, to make 36
Wrapping paper, to save 92
Wreath frame, to save 93
Wreaths, Swags and Logs 40
Writing to Father Christmas 52

Yule Lodge 54-55
Yule Log 40
Yuletide Fashion 27